TO WHOM IT MAY CONCERN

BOOK I

MANY ARE CALLED

by

Nancy, daughter of Helen

Grateful acknowledgment is made to the following and reprinted by permission
of The Putnam Publishing Group from THE COURT MARTIAL OF LT.
CALLEY by Richard Hammer. Copyright © 1971 by Richard Hammer.

Biblical quotations appear from: The Oxford Annotated Bible; and
                                    The Living Bible

Artistic interpretations provided by: Robert Peltz

Published by: Coleman Creek Publishing
                 575 N. Main Street
                 Valentine, NE 69201

Library of Congress Cataloging-in-Publication Data : 98-73838

ISBN:1-57502-944-8

Printed in the USA by

MORRIS PUBLISHING

3212 East Highway 30 • Kearney, NE 68847 • 1-800-650-7888

Dedication

I dedicate this book to my mother, Helen, who was, unquestionably, my greatest earthly teacher.

A Message of Thanks

I wish to thank my beloved husband, Greg, for believing in me. Never once has he doubted the unseen Power that visits me nor my personal responsibility to reach the people of these United States with a dire warning.

I, too, wish to thank my beautiful children, Dave, Bobbi, Chris and Winni for loving me without question and whole-heartedly supporting my efforts to bring about the publication of this book.

I thank my step-sons, Christopher Neil and Andrew Scott for accepting me into their household and loving me for who I am.

There are many others to thank, too; but first and foremost it must be my father and mother-in-law, Henry and Berniece, parents to Greg, without whose wisdom and generous insight I could not have grown. With the gift of advancing years, their minds and hearts have remained ever youthful, wide open and accepting of things little understood; willing to explore endless possibilities.

With great fondness, I say "thank you" to all my grandchildren, Dawn, Erin, Nikili, Steven, Heather and Brian for the wonderful, explorative conversations we have shared and their devoted faith in me as an individual.

I also wish to thank my first husband, Johnny, for allowing me those intervals of time and space when I needed to be alone; alone to write as I was commanded, even though he did not understand the phenomenon that was taking place.

I thank my son, Chris for his analytical scrutiny of the text and professional evaluation; my daughter-in-law, Marian for grammatically critiquing the manuscript; my daughter, Winni for her computer expertise and all the rest of my family, friends and neighbors who have patiently awaited the news contained within this, my first publication.

TABLE OF CONTENTS

INTRODUCTION

The story you are about to read is true. I have no hidden agendas to disguise nor ill purpose in composing the data found in the following pages. It is presented to you as it actually occurred.

What you read may make you a little uncomfortable and provide an undermined feeling of safety within the confines of your own home, church, financial institutions and government. I ask only that you keep an open mind as you approach subject matter which is either new to your thinking or totally foreign to your belief system.

What makes me an expert in producing the material you are about to read?

Nothing. Absolutely nothing.

Why then should you continue to read further?

Because from somewhere in the distance, a "voice" has come forth and made its presence known through telepathic communication. I did not initiate the "phone call"; it did. It has used me as a tool by which to present messages, visions and dreams for a number of years, opening the door for yet another even greater "voice" as the years went by. These communications have been given in hopes that this America will listen to words of acute concern and disappointment in the behavior of our nation and associated political entities.

Do I know who these voices are?

Not exactly.

However, at one point, the greater of these does specify what we may call Him. The lesser of these two voices I have fondly dubbed "The Advocate" as he clearly acts as mediator between the Greater Voice and this nation.

Is this just another way of addressing environmental issues?

Positively not! Much more is at stake.

Dire warnings are being issued telling us that we are at a crossroad in our planetary and spiritual lives. We are being told to make immediate decisions to preserve the health of both ourselves and our planet; time is short.

If these images and voices that have come to me are but a figment of my imagination, then my imagination has run rampant. But the consistency in which the warnings are announced and the very nature by which I am "called" does not allow me to discount their existence. I leave the question of authenticity to you, the reader, and to men and women of the scientific and religious community who may comprehend this phenomenon far better than I.

In the very beginning of this unusual communication, after I was directed to write and record, much of what the Force had to say dealt directly with me; me personally. The Force frequently reiterated that I must take great care in how I relayed information. Mis-information would not be tolerated; not by me! I was cautioned to make love my aim, and that a boastful attitude would not be acceptable. Humility was mandatory.

I was told by this unseen Force that when a message was received, NOT ONE DOT could be changed. So, if the telepathic sentence structure seems oddly written based on today's language use, please understand why.

I'm not perfectly clear why the Force began using the Christian Bible as an additional communication tool, but it has worked well for both of us. This method of communication has provided the Force with a quick way to "speak" and reinstate the words of the Supreme Being of the Old Testament scribes, while providing me, the messenger, with a more leisurely time-frame in which to transcribe already written thoughts.

I have made few references to biblical passages unless they are deemed necessary to enhance the chapter's subject matter; those passages given to me by the Force. Not all Bible presentations were founded in a dynamic manner such as doors being blown open and pages in the Book of Books being tossed about until a passage was selected, or my Bible being thrown to the floor and opening face up with the passage I was to read, but *many* were. It is the more dramatically delivered passages that I feel compelled to record and present to you at this time. The others I will hold for a later date.

The Force hopes to remind us of our original commitment to spirituality and being "one nation under God." At one point, this Force angrily compares the actions of this nation to the actions of another... Israel.

These United States and her people are being reprimanded just as Israel was so long ago. These "voices from a distance" are hastily calling to *all* humanity to come home; return to the one God.

But, for the sake of this book, the Force is concerned only with America and her inhabitants.

I have also been directed by the Force to speak of some of my experiences in life as many of them are what others would consider extraordinary and unusual; even bizarre. These experiences are intended to bring to light many of the events occurring around us everyday, and so often missed. Some of these experiences are from the Light Forces, while others are severely marred by the Dark Side.

In this story, I use three terms to define the manner in which my communication takes place: messages, dreams and visions; each representing a completely different uniqueness for me.

When I speak of messages, I am referring to either a telepathic communication or a passage from the Christian's Bible that these "voices" selected for me. These messages are received while I am awake.

MESSAGES = (received while awake).

Dreams are pictures that come to me while I am asleep; not unlike the same routine that occurs for many of us night after night; however, in this case, I am referring only to those which have been provided by the Force for the purpose of warning.

In the course of these instructive dreams I am often spoken to but, the primary function is to present a message in the form of easy-to-understand pictures. In some instances, I may even find myself actively participating in the unfolding drama; but most of the time, I am merely an observer.

DREAMS = (I am asleep).

Visions are similar to dreams except that they occur while I am awake. I could be quietly sitting at my desk, laying on a grassy knoll staring into the great blue above me, or sitting on my front porch sipping tea when the material world around me slowly transforms into something quite different.

I have no advance knowledge of what scene I may be required to witness. It is entirely possible to find myself confronted by a war scene; the war actually taking place right in front of me. Or, I may find myself viewing a disaster; flood waters rising, an ominous tornado ready to strike; yet, I am fully awake.

During most of these sessions, I am aware of my immediate surroundings. That is to say, if I am sitting on the porch sipping tea, I will be consciously aware of the fact that I am on the porch sipping tea, even though I may be witnessing a nuclear holocaust.

In a vision I am rarely a participate. Therefore, visions could be best described as:

VISIONS = (fully awake although experiencing altered surroundings).

When the Force calls I am given little advance warning of Its approach. In some instances, no notice is given at all; they just arrive.

When I say "they" I am not only referring to the two main telepathic communicators, but also ascribing to the other Beings (or companions) who sometimes accompany the one I call The Advocate.

In the following story not every dream and vision presented is exactly the way it took place. Many have been reduced to more simplified wording without all the descriptives concerning sights and sounds as they were actually witnessed. This was done to ensure the original intent of the warnings without creating reader boredom through continuous dream reviews.

And so... with total acceptance of what I have been asked to do, I take pen in hand to continue my story hoping that we, you and I, can accomplish what the Force has set before us.

Nancy

Chapter 1

A CALL TO WRITE

Many have been called to write. This is not to say that we are all writers; but a force greater than ourselves has called. We are not expected to ask "why"? We are merely expected to obey.

- The Advocate

The above message came to me as I was trying, desperately, to find opening words for this book. I did not know how to explain that I, Nancy, having no more than a High School education, was directed by a Force greater than myself, to bring a message to my fellow Americans.

With the above message, I not only had my opening statement, but felt fairly confident in concluding I was just one of many who had been hand-picked for the job.

Did this conclusion, however, permit me to think that I could cast my duties adrift and leave the other "**many**" to carry on the task alone?

No; not at all.

I knew that each one of us was expected to act in full accord with our individual set of instructions. No assignment was to be left incomplete.

Now faced with the obvious certainty that I have been more than a little slow in bringing my segment of the task to fruition, I feel compelled to state I have never doubted that the Force always expected that I would carry through with my assignment.

Again, if "**Many have been called to write**", this could be the more conspicuous newspaper reporters, magazines editors, script writers, movie directors, or other professional authors. But, I have a distinct feeling that the majority of these heralding voices are coming from less prominent people; those of us referred to as the common man.

1

The Force also stated, "**This is not to say that we are all writers; but a force greater than ourselves has called.**" I would have to agree.

After careful consideration of my task and much reading about others like me, it appears that we are truly, from all walks of life; this motley crew of hand-picked recipients. Some are found to be experienced writers while the rest of us has never published a single item, nor had the desire or inclination to do so.

For those who profess to be writers, the task of coherently putting this material together, under the direction of the Force, poses little problem. However, for those of us who have never experienced authorship, other than the typical articles for our high school or community newspaper, the task is mind-boggling. We don't have a clue as to how we are to begin; we simply know we must.

Among these diverse writers with extraordinary experiences can be found names such as: Annie Kirkwood, Mary Summer Rain, Gordon Michael Scallion, David Moorehouse, Edgar Cayce and Paul Solomon; just to name a few. All these people have (or had) incredible tales to relate concerning their dramatically transformed lives. They, too, became the "tools" through which "**a force greater than ourselves**" could work.

Each one of them has provided us with a clear prognosis for the future. Each one of them has posted notice of impending disaster. They have asked us to look around and "see" what is truly taking place within our own lives and on this planet we call home. Whether we are asked to confront the issue of angels, the Virgin Mary, aliens, Scientific Remote Viewing (SRV), the undisputed wisdom of our Native Americans, misinformation and disinformation from our government, or telepathic communication from somewhere in space, the messages are undeniably the same: "Wake up!"

Other people have been merely poked and prodded along for years before something happens causing them to finally take pen in hand and commit to write. Mine has been the latter.

Being poked and prodded since 1969 is not to say that I purposely ignored the urging of One greater than I. It is to acknowledge, however, that I have been extremely slow in coordinating the many volumes of material necessary for the creation of a proper presentation to the public.

Therefore, I am guilty of withholding information intended for many and sharing it with few.

If I am being directed to address the political, social, moral and environmental misconduct of these United States, then reason projects a strong signal that our worldly neighbors are receiving directives from their own people who have been "**called**" under the watchful eyes of the Force.

My failure to organize the material with some degree of discipline was for a variety of typical human reasons; none of which could be genuinely viewed as excusable. However, in all of this time, I can honestly say that I have never once sensed weariness on the part of the Force as It has waited for me to carry out my prescribed assignment.

Having dealt with this Force openly for many years, I believe It has coached and nurtured me as witness to Its own loving care of all humanity and the beautiful Earth upon which we live. It told me that I was hand-picked to carry a message to the people of the United States, and It has never doubted the accomplishment of Its carefully chosen plan.

At the time I received the above bold-typed message from the Force, I had been mildly complaining to my husband that even though I had received scores of information and was still recording per instructions, I just didn't quite know how to start the story. I needed some sort of jump start... I needed help.

Well, help arrived unexpectedly; although I should not have been surprised.

It was a brisk October day in 1992 which found me attending an all-day conference. We had just paused for a short break, and I was headed back to my office to check on some personnel issues I was hoping had been resolved.

As I hurriedly left the meeting, I was not projecting any one particular thought; my mind was reasonably clear when suddenly, that old familiar voice began to speak:

"**Many have been called to write. This is not to say that we are all writers; but a force greater than ourselves has called. We are not expected to ask 'why'? We are merely expected to obey.**"

I had my opening statement.

Never before had the Force sent telepathic messages to me while I was in my employer's environment. I was thrilled!

Rushing through my office doorway, I excitedly relayed the information to my daughter, Winni, who had been temporarily working in my office.

As I reiterated the words to her, I was ransacking my desk in search of paper and pen in order to record this latest message.

Upon hearing this new message, my daughter expressed concern over my continuous delay in making all this material available to the public as requested by the Force.

I knew she was right.

My mind seriously processed her concern; I agreed that something needed to be done... soon, but merely replied, "I'll think about it."

After the message had been carefully recorded, and somewhat ignoring my daughter's obvious uneasiness, I hurriedly called my husband at his office. I was silently praying that his line would not be busy, or even worse, roll over to his answering machine. I was excited and had great news. I did not wish to speak to his mechanical monster. I needed him; NOW!

The tightness in my neck and shoulders abated as I heard the familiar spiel, "Titan. This is Greg."

The excited words spewed forth from my dry lips with little breath in-between. I was making no sense, and he told me so.

I started over again, more slowly, and spoke with deliberation so as not to waste any more precious time.

My husband laughed when I completed my story and said, "It's pretty bad when you have to be yelled at over all the confusion and commotion of life to make you listen. I think you better get started on that book."

Returning to the conference room was almost unbearable. Now armed with this new message, and the obvious opening statement for the book I had been commissioned to write, I wanted to write. For the remainder of that afternoon I sat through the meeting with half-listening ears. My mind was adrift to places other than the four walls of this meeting arena which now seemed to entomb me.

As I drove home that evening, I was again marveling at the wisdom of the Force. Heading up the access ramp towards the expressway,

I recalled how back in July of this year I had asked my boss for some vacation hours to coincide with the Thanksgiving holidays. At the time, the vacation request was not prompted due to a feeling of urgency concerning messages from the Force; or so I thought. I just felt the need for some quiet; no radio, no TV, no chatter; a change in tempo for my husband and me... the vacation was granted.

Nearing my turn-off, I happily reflected that it was already mid-October. The vacation was a certainty, and now I had the opening statement for my book. In only a few more weeks we would be heading to our ranch to celebrate a time of praise, and I might even get a little writing done.

How could I have ever known that my will was being directed by the Force; that I was merely acting in accordance with its tenancies?

What would have been my clue that this time-slot had been scheduled by "someone else" to assist me in coordinating the multitudes of written material into presentable format?

Who was there to forewarn me that I would be spending my beautiful vacation writing from early morning well into the wee hours of the cold autumn nights?

No one. But write, I did!

Reaching the ranch amidst heavy fog, our eight-hour drive north seemed extremely short. My unseen companions had already placed me in a writing mode and I had been scribbling notes throughout the long drive, scarcely paying attention to the scenery around me.

I remember very little about those first five days and nights at the ranch. I just remember seeing sunlight briefly, then it was night. Night and day blended one into the other until all the notes had been put into order; those for the first book, those for the second, third, etc. My husband prepared most of the meals and left me alone in my secluded world to fulfill my mission.

Having thrust me into this situation, the Force remained my constant companion those many days and nights as I finally took pen in hand to write and assemble just as I had been charged. The persistence of the Force is remarkable. I cannot argue. I simply obey.

Once the vacation was over and we returned home, I found myself often writing from just after dinner until well into the pre-dawn hours of the following day. I wrote feverously due to a drive within me to complete the first book.

Once or twice, I even wrote until it was time to dress and go to work; and yes, I had literally worked all night.

Somehow, though, in those all night sessions, I did not get tired. I was not tired the following day or even the day after. The obligation to write was so strong that I simply could not sleep.

During this period, going to work was almost unbearable due to the compelling urge to write.

These messages are telling us that we have been asleep for a long period of time and that we must wake up. We have become model citizens in a well organized materialistic world where, with cunning, our behavior has been programmed. We are the product of a predetermined, well planned outcome; we have been manipulated. The Force states that we must began to think for ourselves and not be led astray.

This book is an accounting of some of the many hours spent with this Force. The messages are urgent and have been for all too long. They are directed at these United States, its government, and her people.

Chapter 2

THE DIRECTIVE

Write. Record. These things I say to you, write. I say to you, write.

- The Advocate

This directive was given to me in mid-summer, 1969 by an unseen presence after a brief courtship. There had been no warning of his arrival; only his sudden words were my clue.

The day had not been particularly unusual; just a typical, lazy summer day filled with routine gardening chores and a myriad of children's activities.

I had been left seated at the kitchen table to quietly sip the remainder of my iced tea and enjoy the peaceful sounds of a summer evening before clearing the dishes from the table. My husband had retreated to his den, and the children had sprinted outdoors to play in the remaining hours of sunlight.

Simultaneously draining the last drop of tea from the tall, frosted glass and pushing my knotty pine chair back from the table, I slowly rose to begin my nightly task. With several plates neatly stacked in my hands, and thinking of absolutely nothing, I headed toward the sink. I was not even halfway across the linoleum floor when the telepathic voice spoke the above directive.

My mind responded well to this gentle voice. I had actually met him a few weeks earlier. Our meeting was not exactly the kind that one would normally think of in the terms of introductions and hand shakes; no... I never physically saw him. This Being just found his way into my living room one day and began a one-sided conversation while I was in the midst of vacuuming.

Was I frightened?

No; and I cannot explain why; nor why I never doubted my own sanity... I just didn't. His voice was kind and reassuring. None of my senses alerted me to push the panic button. It was as though I had known him before; yet, when I tried to analyze this strange feeling, I could not clearly define a time-frame in human terms.

This puzzled me.

His speech was absolutely captivating; more akin to prose and poetry than great words of wisdom. I was spellbound as I listened to the soothing tones that bore words of incredible love, and thoroughly enjoyed the unconventional way he structured his sentences.

This mysterious voice reminded me of a poet trying to win undying devotion and unconditional love from the object of his affection and I soon came to know that object was me.

I accepted without question.

I was fully aware that this love came from some type of universal source; it was not of this world... the Being gave me to know this. Exactly where the words were originating from I did not know then and still don't know today. He never specified a physical place and I never asked. I suspect it was not an important factor in the Force's overall plan or I would have been told.

What I did know from the very beginning, was that the words were not a thought process originated by me. The sentence structure was odd in comparison to modern-day language usage and I had the greatest sense that I knew him... I knew him!

Even though I continued to puzzle over the nagging thought that I should be able to identify this strange companion, I questioned nothing. I was enthralled, utterly fascinated that he had chosen me to visit.

As the weeks passed, I found myself genuinely disappointed when our little visits were over and I was left alone in a world that seemed less friendly than when he was present. As the disappointment would subside, it was replaced by an inner craving for his presence on a more frequent basis.

I really missed him.

I delayed speaking to my husband about this matter for a variety of reasons: (1) I was enjoying the privacy of this unusual experience, (2) one does not easily blurt these matters out; I needed to collect my thoughts and carefully select my words for a proper presentation, and (3)

I was concerned that once having mentioned this to another human being, my world would dramatically change. I wanted to keep things just the way they were for a little while longer.

In retrospect, it is truly a pity that I do not remember the words that spewed forth during the weeks of that strange courtship. It never occurred to me to write them down, and he didn't instruct me to do so. The Being's love was evident though, and I was completely enamored by my unseen suitor with never a thought to rejection.

It was for all these reasons that I fell into immediate obedience that evening when the tender voice set forth his first set of instructions: **"Write. Record. These things I say to you, write. I say to you, write."**

At that time, even though I had no idea what I was supposed to write, or why, or to whom, I knew from this moment forward I would be expected to have paper and a writing tool close at hand.

His brief courtship had prepared me well for that first commandment. I was neither excited nor questioning. He simply made a statement and I knew I was to obey.

✻ ✻ ✻ ✻

At the beginning of this "other world" courtship, my life was a great deal different than it is now. Married to my first husband, Johnny, I was happily playing the role of wife and mother with thoughts generally consumed by managing a house, actively participating in the customary community activities, and enjoying the lives of four healthy, energetic children. There was little time I could call my own.

My most peaceful and reflective times, however, the times I labeled my own, came when I was cleaning house, gardening or enjoying the quiet of nightfall.

My vocabulary was somewhat limited; I was always asking Johnny for definitions of words.

Perhaps, I was not very mature, but believe my limited vocabulary was a mere reflection of the innocence through which I saw all life. Time, experience, and circumstance have educated the once innocent child.

I was married to the children's father for twenty-five years before we each decided to travel on our own separate roads. Silly pride was our downfall after so many years.

I am currently remarried to another fine gentleman, Greg, and would like to state for the record that neither of these two men ever complained about sharing me with an unseen Force that at times dominated my mind and thinking; a Force that still possesses so much of my heart, also.

For this, I thank them.

So, why did the Force hand-pick and court me?

I don't know.

Was my earlier life so very unusual, giving rise to some sort of pre-selective factor?

I don't believe so.

I cannot be convinced that I was that different from other children.

I remember how it was then, and it has been my observation that many young children and some teenagers do possess an innate ability to see well beyond the learned limitations of their adult counterparts, just as I did.

Do they see angels?

I believe they do.

Did I?

No... at least I don't think so.

Do they see entities from other worlds?

I believe they can.

It is the adults, that over a period of time, teach the child that these things are impossible to view; that they are figments of the child's imagination. The adults soon forget the purity with which they were born and become easily trapped by the acceptable standards of a more modern society.

My mother did not entrap me and place me in a mold of conformity; she was not given to conformity herself. She carefully watched, nurtured and guided me; always answering my questions; never pushing me away. She gave me the freedom to "see" beyond the sight of the normal eye and to "hear" beyond the hearing ear. I was allowed to explore as much as possible.

How do I know about what other children see and hear?

Do I gain this information from a time-honored degree?

No; I do not.

As I stated, it is merely gained through years of observation, whether of my own children or the offspring of friends and neighbors. It is also gained through reading and lively discussions shared with both friends and strangers who are pleased to find a listening ear concerning circumstances that are beyond their comprehension. These people are pleased to speak with an adult who remembers well the whisperings brought to her as a child through an unknown source; the source that gave her to know that more existed than what the physical eyes and ears could detect.

I can relate well to these children of a different mind. From the early age of about three, I knew I was never alone. When I played hide-and-seek, I knew that the only hiding I was doing was from my human friends. A Presence always knew where I was and what I was doing. I knew this; no one told me... I just knew.

While still in grade school, I recall that nighttime was special. I often stood at my bedroom window gazing at the stars with more than idle curiosity. My mind was filled with questions, knowing there was something I was supposed to understand; yet, I could not identify it. My heart and soul just had a hard time remaining "grounded" to this earthly world.

Earth was not my home.

I was given the gift to sing and received a partial scholarship to American University at age eleven and another scholarship to Peabody Conservatory at age fourteen. But I had no aspirations to become a singer. I merely attended these institutions of learning due to the wishes of adults, until it became abundantly clear that the child was not happy.

This was not my goal in life.

It was the dream of others.

I sought a more simplified and quiet life. I just wanted to serve my fellow man and be a good wife and mother. I felt that if I could teach my children brotherly love and they could spread that kind of love to all they met, then I would have done a great deal to better the lot of man.

There were always plenty of neighborhood children to play with, but I preferred being alone. I just never felt like I belonged.

I spent hours as a youth, wandering through the fields of grass and wild flowers, or following the numerous streams as they flowed tantalizingly off into the woods. I counted the trees as my friends. The sky, wind, and tall grasses were my playmates.

So, when this non-human voice made itself known, I readily accepted the relationship. It had the flow of the graceful winds of my youth. It gave me a sense of calm, just like walking through the fields, or following a stream, or wandering into the woods to lie under the canopy of a friendly tree. It seemed to have answered all the questions of the young girl who stared longingly into the night-sky from her bedroom window. It had all the answers to questions she never knew how to ask.

It was a part of me; yet separate.

The Presence that had been with me as a child now had a voice.

Chapter 3

DISTANT BEINGS DEFINED

Over the years, I learned that there were two distinct telepathic communicators and for ease in distinguishing which orator was delivering the message, I began to record them as the Large Voice and Small Voice; later, renaming both. As you will soon see, one is significantly more dramatic in His delivery. Eventually, He did identify Himself.

This Large Voice has a commanding speech that is filled with the hurt and anger of a frustrated parent. He actually seems to weep at times. He refers to himself as "**THE FATHER**" and states "**There is none beside Me.**"

My oldest daughter asked me, "Why do you not just say it is God"?

My reply then and now is simple: "That is not what He said."

He clearly stated, "**I AM THE FATHER. THERE IS NONE BESIDE ME.**" He never once said that He was that which we identify as God; however, at some point He does make reference to His Son.

It is out of respect in identification of this Great One, and not knowing what else I should really do, that any reference made to this particular voice will have all letters capitalized in these writings.

By capitalization, am I then submitting that I agree with my oldest daughter that the "voice" is that of God?

I will let you, the reader, decide.

I am merely stating that I have not been given any specific instructions as to what I am expected to do with this identity, and do therefore, choose to honor this Orator as a Force far greater than the other "voice." I choose to provide loving homage.

The Small Voice is more gentle, most of the time, and seems to play the role of advocate as he attempts to bridge the gap or seal the gaping wound that exists between **THE FATHER**, our America and the people of her land; therefore, I call him The Advocate. But, because I refer to him as the lesser of these two telepathic voices do not underestimate his power.

It is this Advocate who is the gentle companion that accompanies me through the corridors of my many dreams and visions. It is he who helps me to understand what I am seeing. At other times, different Beings accompany him or are sent in his stead, but they do not speak to me.

The messengers who are sent to assist me in dreams and visions are very kind. The Advocate is the one who directs how the message is to be presented. He generally stands slightly behind me, a little to the left or a little to the right. I know when he is there by sensing his presence and/or when a light appears behind me. If I do not understand what they are collectively trying to convey, then the information is presented in another format.

If I still do not understand the message, my teachers simply wait for a more appropriate instance when my comprehension might be on a higher level. It may be days, weeks, months or even years before an attempt is made to repeat a message.

Only once did the Beings ever fully show themselves. On that particular occasion, they were apparently directed to assist me in delivering a short message to mankind, but were not prepared to make their presentation. I had never seen them rush about in such a manner.

In that instance, I suddenly found myself in an empty classroom, starkly painted white. Nothing was there at first; then suddenly there was a scurry of activity and Beings rushed to hold up a large white board on which I was to write... something. Deciding that holding it would not work, they immediately erected some type of easel and promptly placed the board on it. I was then given a writing tool as they stepped back waiting for me to act.

What I was directed to write and my difficulty in transcribing the information is discussed later.

Simply recording the spoken, telepathic message is much easier than trying to understand the visions and dreams. Fortunately, most of the time, I am provided with an instantaneous single word or "knowing" of what is taking place; what is being described.

I, myself, do not recall having ever been addressed by my Christian name when I was "called" to receive messages. A name, as we know it, does not seem necessary to my unseen friends. What I do find interesting, though, is that my mind appears to remain in constant vigilance; carefully monitoring the air waves for any sign of contact by this unknown Force; always ready to serve.

❊　❊　❊　❊

In the beginning, I was not told what I should do with the information once it was received. Originally, the thought of writing a book never actually took form in my mind. I had considered a newspaper column or some type of flyer published by a Christian organization, but never a book.

It seems a bit ridiculous now, but within a few weeks after the command to "**write**" and "**record**", I even wondered if I was just supposed to record the material and carefully seal it up in glass jars or metal containers.

I further wondered if some type of cataclysmic occurrence was about to take place and I had been selected to record events leading up to our physical demise.

I reasoned that, perhaps the storage of this material was necessary in order to be retrieved by a later civilization; just to let them know we were here. And "yes," I was seriously considering the act of burying these glass and metal containers in the backyard of my Georgian home.

The acknowledgment of this simplistic act is embarrassing enough, but after nearly twenty-nine years I must actually face the reality of my total misunderstanding of the importance of these messages; my own naivete.

In Its deep concern for the people of this nation, and delivery of prophetic messages, the Force rarely laughs. It is quite serious. That is not to say that it lacks a sense of humor; for it must have... working with me.

I have experienced moments of incredible joy in Its presence; moments when I felt no direct connection to Earth at all. I would become bathed in Its energy and momentarily transformed to a place completely unknown to me; a place that bore pure love.

I often smile as I wonder how the Force viewed my simplistic thought process... the actual act of burying precious messages It had so methodically scheduled for urgent publication.

Now I find myself giggling at the thought of someone like me out in the backyard, digging a hole to bury treasure for posterity.

Perhaps my unseen friends felt that working with me was going to be a greater challenge than originally anticipated. Or, perhaps they knew the extent of the task before them and were quite willing to be my devoted teachers.

Whatever the case, I was told much later that the collection of written material was to be entitled **"To Whom It May Concern."** I thought this an odd title and pondered the seemingly peculiar choice of words for months.

By this action, I was truthfully questioning the decision made by the Force.

If they wanted me to write a book, I reasoned, how would I ever get people to consider a publication with a title like that? I could not understand why anyone would entitle a book with a greeting that addresses an unknown entity... a "no one in particular" or a "whoever chooses to read this" sort of heading.

Seated at my desk one night around midnight, still unable to comprehend the reason for this title choice, my Bible abruptly fell from the desk to the floor beneath.

I had not touched it.

I simply heard the unopened Book of Books hit the floor and saw it open, face up.

Only seconds before this event, I had once again been stewing over what I deemed, an inappropriate title selection and how foolish it made me feel.

With very little thought being given to the book now lying on the floor, or what had caused it to fall, I rather absentmindedly leaned over in my chair and carefully retrieved it.

As the "who" and "why" still swirled around within my head, I placed the opened book on the desk in front of me and immediately began to sense a need to read... something.

Patiently waiting, I realized that my mind had been called into action and had already requested the eyes to search the open pages for some degree of instruction.

The eyes were rapidly scanning the two open pages in a systemic fashion, when suddenly they found the appointed passage required for my immediate lesson. I was told:

Son of man, I have made you a watchman for the house of Israel; whenever you hear a word from my mouth, you shall give them warning from me. If I say to the wicked, 'You shall surely die,' and you give him no warning, nor speak to warn the wicked from his wicked way, in order to save his life, that wicked man shall die in his iniquity; but his blood I will require at your hand. But if you warn the wicked, and he does not turn from his wickedness, or from his wicked way, he shall die in his iniquity; but you will have saved your life. Again, if a righteous man turns from his righteousness and commits iniquity, and I lay a stumbling block before him, he shall die; because you have not warned him, he shall die for his sin, and his righteous deeds which he has done shall not be remembered; but his blood I will require at your hand. Nevertheless if you warn the righteous man not to sin, and he does not sin, he shall surely live, because he took warning; and you will have saved your life. (Ezekiel 3:17-21)

My vision became blurry before I had even finished the reading, and I could scarcely see the last few lines. I began recording the biblical selection as tears trickled down my cheeks and fell abruptly into droplets creating tiny splashes on my paper. The newly penned words quickly joined forces with these wee puddles, as ink and tears became one.

I would grumble no more. It was not Israel for whom I was to be a watchman; it was America. I was clearly charged with the task of being my brothers' keeper; keeper of the inhabitants of these United States. Failure to warn those that the Force dearly loved would produce dire circumstances for this entity known as Nancy.

I had my answer. It was certainly not the one I had been looking for; but the Force was not soliciting suggestions from one of the **"many"** It had called into service. There was no need for more questions. I would no longer ask "who" or "why." I would simply write, record and present the material as I had been instructed.

At another point in time, I had been additionally advised that the language I chose to use in writing the book was to be kept simple. I was to remain ever mindful of our language and not use elaborate words. My writings were to be directed more for what was termed the "common man" and their respective children; everyone needed to understand what was happening.

Chapter 4

MYSTERIOUS VISITORS

I believe this story actually begins a year before the command was given to "**write**" and "**record**." It appears that the Force had been trying to get my attention in a less than subtle way through the appearance of a mysterious Being who first came as a Comforter to a hospital bedside, and then came again, the following summer as a Giver of Life when he rescued of my youngest son.

That August, 1968 evening was hot and muggy as I dragged my tired body out onto the screen porch to embrace some cool breezes. Yard work and gardening in the sweltering heat had taken its toll on my poor body. Supper had been late, but at least the children were ready for bed. My first husband, Johnny, offered to "tuck the children in" when their respective bedtimes arrived.

I nodded my head in grateful approval and agreed with him that the children could play in their rooms a little longer while we discussed some of the day's events.

Soon our youngest son, Chris (age 6), came out onto the porch complaining that his older sister, Pam (age 8), would not play with him; she was being mean!

We told him to go back to the bedroom and tell her to play nicely.

He acknowledged, and departed with much sadness.

A few moments later, a dejected Chris was back *again* complaining. He was angry because Pam wouldn't answer him. She was just laying under her bed making funny noises.

At this point, Johnny decided it was past time for the younger children to be in bed anyway. He left the porch to put them in bed as my mind drifted away on one of those cool, summer breezes meandering up from the creek.

My thoughts were suddenly jolted back to reality as Chris came bursting out onto the porch, excitedly stating, "Daddy wants you in Pam's room."

My mind and body stiffened.

I panicked!

My husband never sent the children after me when he wanted something; he always came himself!

Gathering my wits about me, I ran to Pam's bedroom where I found Johnny propping her up on her bed.

Her eyes were open, but had rolled back in her head so that only the whites were visible. She appeared to have a substance like sea foam around the edges of her mouth, and was making peculiar guttural sounds.

"What happened!" I gasped.

"I don't know," Johnny said, obviously perplexed. "I found her partially under the bed hidden by her blanket when I came to tuck her in."

Frightened, I quietly called her name, "Pam?"

"She can't hear you, Hon," Johnny said with great concern, "Call an ambulance and get a doctor, quick!"

Panic struck again!

I raced back to the kitchen where I literally ran back and forth between the phone directory and the telephone itself, totally incapable of functioning intelligently.

We had just moved from another state. WE HAD NO DOCTOR YET!

Seconds later, Johnny came dashing into the kitchen with Pam's limp body draped over his arms.

I was still running around in a total state of shock.

"There's no time! We'll have to take her ourselves," he said as he kicked open the screen door that led directly to the carport.

Chris was screaming hysterically, "What's wrong with Pam? What's wrong with Pam?"

He was so upset and we weren't making things any easier for him with our own excitable reactions to the situation at hand.

With all the commotion taking place, our oldest boy, David (age 12), came into the kitchen to see what was going on. I frantically called to him to go next door and get the neighbor lady to come stay at the house with Chris and his youngest sister, Winni, our 3-year old. He immediately disappeared to retrieve help.

Getting Pam into the station wagon was a near impossibility. Her limp body was so flexible that it seemed to defy our urgent attempts to grasp it firmly.

At last, her small body snuggled tightly between my arms and lap, we tore out of the driveway with horn blowing and car lights flashing.

Pam went into convulsions.

We raced through stop signs and traffic lights, frantically dodging vehicles that got in our way.

No police car could be found to help us.

Pam's convulsions were getting stronger and her whole body was becoming rigid. It took all my strength to hold on to her as our vehicle raced through the night. My muscles ached.

Reaching the hospital, Johnny slammed on the brakes, leaped out of the station wagon and ran to my side of the car where he struggled to take Pam's rigid body from my arms.

She was turning blue!

We both ran through the main entrance of the hospital, completely missing the sign that would have directed us to the emergency room. Pointing fingers guided us down the proper corridor to a nurse who dashed towards us with a formidable looking cart.

When Johnny placed Pam on the gurney, her knees flew up in one great convulsion and remained fixed to her forehead.

The nurse was quickly joined by other staff members as they whisked her away.

Numbness was setting in as we paused to catch our breath when suddenly, Johnny remembered that the car lights were on and the motor still running. He left to take care of these material necessities only to find that some kind soul had already tended to them.

Returning to where I stood in the hallway, outside Pam's emergency room, his knees gave way and he nearly sank to the floor. I grabbed for him as he reached for the corridor wall.

"Must have been all that running," he said. But my heart ached for him as I knew full well the grief his body and mind felt toward this helpless child of his.

Time meant nothing. We were in a complete void. I could not ask "Why?" I could not even find the words to pray. I do not even remember what we did, where we sat, if we sat, or what we said during that miserable wait.

Finally, after three and a half hours, a doctor stepped from Pam's secluded room and said, "We think she'll be alright. We lose more children that way. We had to give her more medication than we normally give an adult under these conditions..."

I don't know what else he said. It suddenly seized me that her precious life had nearly slipped away.

The doctor told us we could see her briefly while a room was being prepared for her hospital stay.

As we headed toward her emergency room door, I remained in a complete stupor. I was merely placing one foot in front of the other only because I knew that's what you had to do in order to walk; I was supposed to this.

As we walked toward that little body on the emergency room table, there was no way anyone could have prepared me for what I was about to see.

"Oh, my God!" I tearfully gasped, "She doesn't even look like my own child!" I heard myself cry in a heightened state of shock once again.

My mind quickly ran backwards remembering the talkative youngster with an unquenchable appetite for knowledge that had been mine only hours before. I could see her short, curly, golden brown hair flash with red highlights as she flipped her head from side to side while discussing whatever delighted her fancy. Her eye-lids would blink swiftly while she was in deep conversation, and her green eyes flash with enthusiasm. Her contagious laugh won the hearts of those she encountered as she cheerfully displayed her tiny dimple.

Born without a single physical defect, her skin provided her with a healthy glow while her small, delicate frame revealed the inherited characteristics of her paternal grandmother.

Now her beautiful green eyes were tightly sealed in a deep sleep. The once lively eye-lids were a greenish-purple and black, and she had bruises all around her ears and cheeks. Her lovely, smooth skin was eerie white and slimy. Her beautiful wheat-colored tresses had been replaced by what appeared to be a tangled mass of smelly seaweed.

She wrestled unconsciously for every breath. Mucous could be heard rattling in her throat with every exhaled breath as she struggled to maintain her own life forces.

The doctor spoke again to us explaining the reasons for her appearance, but I remember so little. My fractured mind was too far gone to hear. I could only see my once healthy child reduced to near decay.

The hospital was kind enough to provide me with a bed in Pam's room so I could remain with her that night and try to get some sleep. Johnny went home to relieve the friendly neighbor who had been placed in charge of our other children.

Later that night, as I sat on the edge of my temporary bed, I found that all human thought had deserted me. I just stared in numbness at the pathetic scene that was before me.

Not a single prayer could be found. I could only see the rails on the bed that were keeping my child's tortured body from falling out, some type of breathing machine and a kind-faced Florence Nightingale, who was carefully watching, listening and monitoring the ailing body.

As I continued to gaze in numbness, and watch that lonely bed, a strange series of events began to unfold.

Slowly, I became aware of a Presence behind me.

I knew it was not of this world.

I was not afraid.

It was gently trying to calm me, and show me something.

I was numb from the shock of all that had taken place and desperately clung to the strength that this Presence so generously provided.

My attention was being directed towards my daughter as a vision began to emerge.

VISION... **The metal bed rails that are confining the small, tortured body of my daughter to the length and width of the hospital mattress seem to be disintegrating. The noisy breathing machine is slowly fading into oblivion. The nurse is disappearing as though consumed by an invisible mist.**

I am not confused. My unseen companion does not allow the existence of confusion. I simply feel warm and secure under the protection and strength of this Force, and I rest. He seems to cover me in a blanket of love as he shows me that all illness has left this child of mine.

Pam's hair is no longer wet and smelly, but lies in lovely silken folds around her head and shoulders. Her

23

face hides its clammy white and is replaced with a rosy hue. The strangling has ceased. Her eyelids are no longer grotesquely discolored, but look peaceful as though she is only resting. The pillow under her head is like a fleecy white cloud and her bed seems made of soft, white, fluffy cotton.

As I watch, a pale glow gradually develops in the shape of an arc from the crown of her head to her now peaceful chest.

Within this silence a single telepathic word emerges: "PERFECT."

I am considering this word as the vision begins to fade bringing back the previous condition where illness prevails.

The vision is now gone and so is my mysterious companion, my Comforter.

I gave much thought to what I had witnessed and, with the rising sun, felt I knew what it all meant.

I was told that this child was "**Perfect**" in the sight of God. Whether she lived or died was not the issue. The truth was that He was with her now and for always, as He is with all of us.

In the beginning she had been created perfect, her existence was eternal, her human form was only temporary.

When my husband arrived the next morning, I found great difficulty in explaining the course of events that had befallen me. How could I possibly tell this man, who called himself a religious "fence sitter," an agnostic, the wondrous things I had just witnessed? How could I tell him that it did not matter whether his daughter lived or died; that she would always belong to God Almighty, her Creator, when I was not even sure I understood myself?

Pam recovered rapidly, as most children do. The doctors found no cause for this peculiar health episode but decided to treat her as an epileptic.

My mind replayed the memory of my unseen friend and the vision he gave me for months. I did not choose to analyze it, I just wanted to experience it over and over again.

❊ ❊ ❊ ❊

Nearly a year had passed since Pam's ordeal when my parents invited themselves to visit our new home in Georgia; the time being early July, 1969.

Having only been through this southern state on their way to Florida for vacations, they planned a more leisurely trip, this time, to coincide with their latest rock hounding expedition into the Carolina mountains and pink marble quarries of Georgia. The children and I were then invited to join them on their return excursion; back home to Maryland.

We gratefully accepted and excitedly looked forward to moderate adventures in the exploration of bright, colored gemstones.

Our first stop was to seek sapphires. It was a hot, dirty, stinky and tiresome job. We were discouraged, but the next day of searching for garnets in a cool mountain stream in North Carolina was refreshing, fun, and profitable.

Later that same day, we called our treasure hunt to a halt and drove to a group of log cabins where we planned to spend the night.

With still ample time before dinner, we wandered haphazardly around the freshly cut, sparsely turfed, green lawn and spoke with some of the other cabin inhabitants.

One tall, lanky gentleman from Kentucky began talking to my Mom about "divining rods."

I was listening in on their conversation when I heard him say he'd "be pleased to show us" how he found water for folks in the mountains where he lived.

He called himself a "water witcher" and said when he and his "stick" located a specific spot where water could be found, folks would dig their wells right where the stick pointed.

"Always works," I heard him say.

My Mom was excited over the old concept of which she had heard much, and called us to join her. We proceeded to follow this stranger to the edge of a wooded area where many saplings grew. There he selected a young tree for his purposes, cut it down, trimmed it to size and proceeded with his demonstration.

With the bottom of this "Y" shaped sapling pointing straight up to the sky he began walking around the lawn, then headed towards the creek. In so doing, I noticed that this young tree was beginning to move in a slightly downward motion. I was not sure that I was really seeing a movement or whether I was merely caught up in an expectation of a promise made.

Moving closer, and walking along side him, I realized that it was not my imagination. The closer he got to the creek the more the sapling bent and twisted so that the portion that started out in an upright position, that portion that pointed straight up to the sky, was now moving steadily downward.

I watched intently, as the sapling pulled itself down so that by the time the Kentuckian reached the water's edge, the naked, young tree pointed straight down at the water. The muscles in the man's hands and arms strained as he held firmly onto this piece of wood that seemed to come to life.

Doubting what I had just witnessed I heard myself say, "I'd like to try."

Obligingly, I was handed this water hungry sapling and instructed how to hold it.

I backed all the way up near our cabin and began following the roadway, just in case something strange might be lurking under the lawn to cause this sapling to behave in such a peculiar manner.

Much to my shock, the results were the same.

What an odd feeling to have this stick, this stripped tree, this young wood that was severed from its very foundation, come alive in my hands. It's desire to point downward, down towards the water was so acute that I had to strain to maintain a firm hold.

And so the rest of the family members tried in succession; all but my Dad. Watching closely, I observed that this sapling worked better, with a greater degree of intensity, for some more than others. Even though Chris was small and young, this divining rod seemed to behave differently for him than the rest of us. It seemed to behave more powerfully with the same magnitude as it did for the Kentuckian.

While I continued to speak with this stranger concerning other matters, Mom scurried off to prepare our meal.

I joined her later.

Soon, picnic foods were prepared and each child was given a choice as to where he or she wanted to eat. Pam and Chris quickly raced to a table near the creek. Winni chose the front porch steps of her grandparents' cabin, while David disappeared with his bag of tasty morsels and was nowhere in sight as Mom, Dad and I prepared to sit down.

26

As I pulled up a chair to join my parents, I glanced, one more time, at the two children down by the creek to make sure everything was all right.

I saw Pam begin to swat at something with her hands, and since her table of choice was close to the water's edge, and the coolness of the evening was settling in, I assumed that she might be having some difficulty with mosquitoes. So, I turned away.

"What's wrong with the children?" Mom asked staring intently passed me.

Then I heard blood-curdling screams. I turned to see Pam leap off her bench and run to Chris who was screaming hysterically and flailing his arms wildly.

I dashed off the porch to attack an unknown assailant.

Chris was screaming uncontrollably and yelling, "My foot! My foot!" when I reached him. Even though the air around us was full of wasps, I had no idea what he was talking about. His high-top sneakers should have protected his ankles and feet.

The angry wasps were everywhere as I swatted in all directions with haste and speed.

Suddenly, I saw two of them on the top of Chris' cloth shoe, stinging him at ankle height. They would not release him. I hit at them again and again with my bare hands and finally knocked them off without getting stung myself.

Chris was now rolling on the ground kicking his feet frantically and screaming so violently that he was gasping for air. His voice was becoming inaudible; his hair covered in sweat. I could not fathom what was taking place!

I grabbed at his shoelaces, trying desperately to loosen the knots and release his feet. Once past the shoes, I made another grab for the wildly flying feet and yanked off the socks.

"Oh, my God!" I cried softly when I saw the many stings surrounding his ankles which were swelling at an *incredible* rate. "I need help!" my stunned mind squeaked in desperation to an unknown Force.

I was afraid for my son!

Before I even uttered these words, out of the corner of my eye I had caught the glimpse of a middle-aged gentleman racing across the lawn towards us as I held Chris on the ground struggling with his shoelaces.

Upon his arrival, the man initiated a conversation with me and without even looking up, I replied while studying Chris' ankles.

I do not recall what he said that prompted a reply. I just remember this calm-voiced gentleman breaking a tiny glass vial between his fingers and rubbing small amounts of something on each sting and the surrounding area as he spoke.

He said, "Your son will be just fine, but make sure you take him to see his doctor when you get home."

"We're on vacation," I nervously replied, "and won't be back home for another ten days."

My eyes were still on Chris' ankles; the swelling was already subsiding.

"That will not be a problem; he will be fine. But make sure that you take him to see his doctor just as soon as you get back home," he repeated.

"Thank you very much," I said without looking up, "I will."

I sat with Chris on the grass for a long time until he appeared calm enough for me to leave him momentarily. Then I told him I was going to talk to his sister, Pam, who was very worried about him.

"Is that OK?" I asked, to see if he was calm enough for me to leave.

"Yeah," he sniffed as he wiped his teary eyes and runny nose with the backs of his small, dirty hands.

I left to check on Pam.

Poor Pam.

She had never uttered a word of complaint; she had only raced to the other side of the picnic table to help her younger brother; and yet, she too, had been stung numerous times on one arm alone. She was in tears, but not for herself. She was in tears because she was unable to provide her brother with the help he so desperately needed.

Upon further scrutiny of the table area, I noticed that there were many wasps flying around irritably and realized the kids had somehow disturbed their nest. It was on the underside of the table.

Time passed; we all recovered; however, the picnic mood was definitely destroyed. I told my Mom I wanted to find the doctor who helped us and thank him for his kindness. I was also curious about the wonder drug contained in that tiny glass vial that so instantaneously eased the pain and swelling in my son's ankles.

Mom agreed that I should go and said that she would take care of the children while I was gone. I asked Mom if she had seen the doctor, and if she knew which cabin he was staying in.

She said "Yes," she had seen him, but "No," she had no idea where he came from.

This man I was looking for was of average build as I recall, although I really didn't get a very good look at him. His trousers were brown and he wore a white shirt with a tie. His hair was more brown than gray and that's all I could remember.

I suspected he had driven here for a short vacation and had not even had a chance to change his clothing.

I proceeded to the cabin where I first caught a glimpse of the doctor running towards Chris. A lady came to the door. Her reply to my inquiry was brief. She stated that she was the only occupant of that particular cabin.; however, when "all the commotion started" she did remember seeing a gray-haired man run across the grass in front of her cabin, and did see him doing something to the young boy who was crying. That's all she knew.

I thanked her for her time and proceeded to the next cabin; and the next, and the next, and so on, until I had covered every cabin in the complex. None of the men I saw resembled the man who had come to my son's aid.

I discovered there were *no* doctors, paramedics, or any type of emergency medical technicians among this group of vacationers. Everyone I spoke to, who had witnessed the incident, remembered quite clearly the middle-aged gentleman who responded to the agonized screams of a young boy, but *no one* had any idea where he came from.

They all remembered suddenly seeing him in front of one of the cabins or running to Chris' aid, but no one even remembered seeing the man leave after treating Chris.

He was just there one minute and gone the next.

This "man" brought no black medical bag; he just had one tiny glass vial. I had actually seen the swelling and redness disappear before my very own eyes.

I had cried out for help, and help arrived. The sound of his voice had given hope and encouragement to an anxious mother.

A young boy screamed in pain and fright, and the pain and fright were banished.

When we got back to Georgia, I did as the mysterious man had instructed me and took Chris to our pediatrician. It was determined that Chris was highly allergic to bee stings and that I would have to keep some Benadryl on hand at all times as *a single sting could possibly cause him heart failure.*

The pediatrician said that we were awfully lucky to have a doctor on hand to assist in the middle of nowhere, and "no," he could not be certain what might have been in the tiny glass vial.

Was my middle-aged gentleman with the soft, comforting voice the same Force of unknown origin that came to me when Pam was so ill? I really don't know; but a huge "thank you" was definitely in order.

Thanks for saving my son's life "doc," whoever you are, and wherever you came from.

Chapter 5

THE CRASH COURSE

The drive from North Carolina to Maryland had been tedious. I was tired and did not know why. Maybe it was due to all the recent excitement, but I could not be sure. Even while en route to Mom and Dad's house, I had actually gotten quite dizzy a couple of times, necessitating a change in drivers. No longer could I be counted as a safe driver with this new malady.

Mom drove my car and kept an eye on my wandering health while Dad took the lead to guide us homeward. I didn't feel sick; I just didn't feel "all together." Something was very different and I couldn't determine the cause. I slept most of the time, being continuously bombarded by what seemed to be, prophetic dreams. I chose to analyze this situation later.

Once at Mom and Dad's house we set aside all thoughts of our recent rock hounding adventures, and placed our stone treasures in a secure place. Much sorting of these gems still needed to be done for quality and possible sales, but we simply set them aside for further scrutiny at a later date. The children and I were here to rest and play, and I, in particular, seemed to be in dire need of that rest.

It was nice to visit with my folks again in the confines of their own home. A concrete swimming pool took up much of the backyard and provided the children with an outlet for their ample energies.

I found a comfortable chair under the protection of a well-worn patio umbrella beside the pool. Sliding into the lounge chair, I wiggled slightly in my seat to obtain a better position and glanced around with pleasure at the familiar sights; I was so tired.

The scene from the pool arena was refreshing with tall, thin, loblolly pines, youthful trees of maple, wide-spreading dogwood, spindly-armed redbud and a few orange-colored wild azaleas, and of course, wild rose bushes. This miniature forest contained many small creatures, including birds, squirrels and rabbits. The most popular of these creatures being a Mocking Bird my father had fondly named "Knuckle Head." I have no idea why.

I got up and moved my chair closer to the edge of the sparkling blue waters where the children were at play. The sound of their laughter was like a symphony and soon my mind drifted away to the lanky Kentuckian and his divining rod. I saw vividly everything he had done and wished that I could better grasp the phenomenon behind that special tool; that special gift.

Time lapsed, and I fell asleep.

Soon I awakened with a start for I had just witnessed a re-run of the action taken by the "doctor" who assisted us near the log cabins. My mind did not provide me with a retake of the portion involving a crying child, but instead, placed me on the lawn where the "doctor" had instantly materialized.

He had done exactly that; he had materialized, already in a running position.

I was stunned!

After that revelation, it took me a while to fall back to sleep; but sleep I did. At some point, I gradually emerged from my deep slumber with an acute awareness that the symphonic sounds of my sleep state were turning to pure noise due to some kind of bustling activity. I awakened to a noticeable change in my surroundings.

Mom had phoned friends and neighbors to entice them to come over for a dip in the pool, a buffet-style picnic, and a "see Nancy and the grandchildren." Many had accepted the invitation and folks were in the process of arriving. It was good to see so many old, familiar faces and catch up on the latest details in their lives.

Mom and Dad's friends had always been kind and polite people, and not wanting to stay too long, began leaving around eight o'clock that evening. The day had been good, the children had enjoyed themselves immensely, and now it was time for bed.

Mom and I did not retire so quickly though, and ended up talking into the wee hours of early morning. I don't remember when we finally climbed into bed, but I am sure that sunrise was not far away.

I slept well that night, and in the morning became dimly aware that the children were up and roaming throughout the house. As I lay in a semi-conscious state, mindful of life's sounds around me, I drifted to a place that was devoid of all greenery. And so, a dream began:

> *DREAM*... **I find myself outdoors in a relatively small area that seems rather sandy; similar to a desert, due to its lack of vegetation.**
>
> **My attention is being drawn to look upward towards a small cliff to my left and move a little closer to its base.**
>
> **Moving forward, a string suddenly appears which is secured to the top of the cliff and extends all the way down to within inches of the ground, just a few feet in front of me. The line has a pointed metal object at the end which keeps the string taut. However, I find it strange that the line is not straight.**
>
> **A voice begins to speak, but its message is drowned out by my own excited interruption as I recognize the tool being used.**
>
> **"Oh, I know what that is!" I exclaim as my body twitches in excitement.**
>
> **As I blurt out these words, I am directed to remember an Old Testament story about the prophet Amos.**

I had readily recognized the instrument. The line with a metal object at the end is called a plumb line (or plumb bob as my dad used to call it). My dad had often used this tool to establish vertical lines when he built houses and retaining walls. I had assisted him on several occasions.

I understood the meaning of the dream for I remembered well the lesson given to Amos, but chose to look it up anyway. The passage states the following:

> **He showed me: behold, the Lord was standing beside a wall built with a plumb line in his hand. And the Lord said to me, "Amos, what do you see?" And I said, "A plumb line." Then the Lord said, "Behold, I am setting a plumb line in the midst of my people Israel; I will never again pass by them."** (Amos 7:7-8)

I knew it was my America and her inhabitants that were being measured this time; not Israel. We were way out of alignment. America was being measured and found wanting. We were "crooked," we were not standing "straight."

I also knew that His warning was directed more toward our leaders than the populace; but, the populace was not excluded from the warning. The entire nation was going to "topple over" if we continued on our current path.

The sandy, desert environment pictured with this message was to show that we are being "laid to waste." We are not only destroying ourselves, but are willing to allow others to aid in our destruction.

Being reminded of the prophet Amos and the situation we both were called to witness, was not the last of my lessons that day. As I was drifting off to sleep once again, I was told to "rest."

My unseen friends explained to me that the exhaustion I was experiencing was not a genuine tiredness, not a mental or physical weariness; but, rather an induced sleepiness. They (the Force) had much to communicate and preferred that I be in a "sleep state" for better contact. Hence, it was "they" who were inducing this sense of weariness; this dizzy/drugged state which was compelling me to sleep.

So, the lessons continued that morning with many exciting things shown to me but, I cannot say I always understood the context.

I felt like a willing participant in some sort of educational "crash course," and I didn't even remember enrolling in the class. The exhaustive process was most intriguing.

At times, I was extremely confused and felt like I needed an entirely new set of encyclopedias for reference. This set of encyclopedias would have to be extraordinary; nothing produced by the current, working knowledge of humans; but, one assembled by these Beings of remarkable intelligence.

The dreams resumed:

DREAM... **I am being warned of a disastrous flood that will soon begin. I realize that "soon" is a relative term and know these flood waters will not cover the entire world as they once did during the Old Testament time of Noah. However, they will cause great suffering and destruction with widespread damage.**

Enormous numbers of animals, birds of the fields and fish will perish; some species never to be seen again. Incredible numbers of our own kind will disappear during this purging, while crops in the fields will be a total failure.

When a colossal, menacingly eerie, dark black cloud arises from beyond the distant hill, I call out in a desperate voice to my family and friends and gather them together in the safety of a house, leaving the front door ajar. They are not pleased that I have disturbed their "party" but reclaim their playful mood once they enter the shelter of this dwelling.

I am not sure where I am, but the surroundings are familiar. The streets near this house are extremely narrow and made of small cobblestones. The buildings are smooth as though made of dried mud, yet white in color. The doorways are rounded at the top and there are two stone steps at the front entrance, much like the white marble steps of the old row-houses in Baltimore, Maryland.

There are overhead archways spanning the pebbled streets that are connected near the lower roof-line of the houses with no apparent supports extending down to the streets.

In a less-than-calm manner, I find myself giving everyone in this house instructions on how to save themselves when the rains come, causing severe flooding. I tell them to save their cereal.

Yet, in spite of my urgent warnings, they pay no heed and continue in their festive mood; eating, drinking and laughing.

I am aghast!

I see ominous, tumbling, fearfully black clouds appear three times, dousing the warm Earth heavily, as I peer through the partially open doorway. I walk dejectedly outside and sit down on the top step, weeping for my family and friends. My stomach is churning.

Why won't they listen to me?

The rains cease as I continue to listen to the gaiety which flows from within this house. I weep even harder for the lack of understanding that is mine to deal with. I have so much to tell these people and they will not even consider the simple things I tell them. "Save your cereal," I have warned. But they will not listen.

I do not want them to perish. I want my husband and children to survive! I want my friends to survive! I want mankind to survive!

Suddenly the air is electrified as a great lightening bolt strikes the ground about a foot away from my right side and next to the stone stairs on which I sit.

I am to weep no more.

I can hear the crackle of high tension from the voltage in this powerful object. The dazzling, yellowish-white bolt nearly blinds me as it stands, quivering, with its point only fractions of an inch above the wet ground near my right foot.

I know I am being told I must return to the people and try again to make them understand. I do not have time to waste. I do not have time to weep.

I lift my weary body from the hard, stone steps to make my way back into the house; to make my warnings known amidst the party atmosphere that plays like a sad melody in my mind.

The lightening bolt does not move. It remains as a steady reminder that I must continue as instructed. I have work to do. I must enter the "house" (America) and speak to the "people" (the Americans). They must be warned. Time is running out.

Again, the people in this house will not listen to me. Their party mood does not lend itself to listening to a "bearer of bad tidings."

Turning away from this carefree atmosphere, I head back outside to the fresh morning air, making a conscious decision to try again, later. In great sadness, I meander down the rigid, cold steps to the warmth of the soil below.

The scene now changes, and I find myself near an ordinary, metal rubbish can where I am about to dispose of a small amount of trash. Strangely, a tiny pebble on the wall beside the can catches my eye as it flashes with a red brilliance.

I quickly dispose of the trash and, pleased with my discovery, gently pick up my tiny treasure with thoughts of taking this pretty pebble to my parents for their rock collection.

With great interest, I examine the specimen and suddenly realize I am now in possession of a bright red ruby. How strange!

Upon even closer examination, the pebble grows into a stone tablet two inches square. As I watch, the shape and color change simultaneously. Now it has turned gray with white specks, resembling a piece of granite. A chiseled drawing then appears which I know to be some type of sign, but I cannot fathom its meaning.

I am directed to look at the hills to my right, off in the distance, where I see Stone Mountain with her ever-busy, enclosed skylifts transporting people to the top. I know that each lift is capable of carrying fifty passengers. There are also open seats, like a typical ski lift, with people crowded onto them. These too, are heading to the top and I feel this to be rather odd as I have no recollection of such chairs in use at Stone Mountain.

Again, I note another oddity: no one is descending. People are only ascending; ascending, silently and peacefully, in great numbers.

How peculiar!

I have a feeling that if I strenuously focus my eyes in that same direction, beyond Stone Mountain, I will find the answer to the tablet drawing, for whatever reason. However, try as I may, I am unable to identify anything that even remotely resembles my chiseled drawing. I still do not understand!

Seeing nothing, and in sheer frustration, I give the tiny stone tablet a careless toss where it lands on the pebbled street just outside the city walls.

Once again, with heavy heart, I begin walking away, down the dirt road, heading out of town, leaving this grievous city behind.

My frustration level has left me with a blank mind as I walk away from this partying city. Scuffing up dust and dirt with my shoes as I walk away, I cannot help but to continue scanning the distant hills for some kind of an answer to my riddle.

Squinting profusely, I strain to recognize something that brings a vague recollection.

Then I know!

On top of one hill stands a huge stone similar to those at Stonehenge but carved exactly like the left half of my chiseled drawing; my stone tablet. A little further over to the right is another hill with a similar stone structure, only carved like the second half of my chiseled drawing.

I'm so excited!

Suddenly I hear my mother say in a calm voice, "Yes, Nancy, yes."

Looking to my father with eagerness and the hope of some type of explanation, he simply smiles and stands quite still; a typical reaction from my father.

The two of them slowly vanish into thin air; they are only apparitions.

Where did my parents suddenly come from? What do they know that I do not? With irritation, my mind screams, "I DO NOT UNDERSTAND!"

Back to the city I race, feeling that I must find the tiny stone tablet with the precious drawing!

In a state of panic, I search feverously throughout the city street where the stone tablet was tossed, but cannot find it.

All the stones look alike.

As I search over and over, I feel sick as I realize the streets have been swept clean by the growing Frightening Force, and know I will never find it.

In a more awakened state, I remember thinking that to tell the people to save their "**cereal**" sounded a little silly. I wondered whether I should take so literally the present day usage of this term referencing a breakfast food and decided to turn to the wisdom of Mr. Webster for further clarification.

According to Webster's dictionary the word "**cereal**" comes from the French (cereale) or from Latin (cerealis) both of which mean grain; or relating to grain or the plants that produce it.

It then became quite obvious by this explanation, that we were being told to save our grain, and by blending this new dream with other little messages that had been thrown at me on this trip, I had a rather startling picture.

America is being told that she will need all the grain she can store to keep her own inhabitants from starvation. Just as in the biblical story of Joseph, where he saved the Pharaoh's people from starvation due to a seven-year drought, we too, are headed for severe shortages and have been warned. It is entirely up to us whether we choose to take the necessary steps of preparation to survive or not.

In other dreams presented to me, while Mother was driving my car back from North Carolina, my friends informed me that our food shortages will not be caused by drought at first; but, too much water (flooding) which will inhibit planting and harvesting. They said these floods will badly affect our grain production.

Rain, hail, tornadoes, hurricanes and heavy snows will come at most unpredictable times causing wide-spread damage. Many of these weather devastations will occur in areas that have previously been unaffected by such things.

After the unprecedented period of floods, I am told the droughts will begin. A mixture of severe drought and torrential rains will then linger for an undetermined time-frame causing huge dust storms or wet, soggy land, depending upon where you live. The grain belt of our nation will not fully recover soon enough to meet the demands of both people and livestock before the huge, major catastrophe hits the west coast in form of earthquake induced land loss and volcanic action.

I was also told, our grain houses are not full and we are poorly prepared, regardless of what we may hear from the economical and political circles.

We are advised to prepare for when the waters come; when disaster strikes. We are told to put away a stock of grains to save ourselves and our livestock.

The party time is over.

More serious tasks are at hand.

We cannot depend on someone else to provide for us.

40

In the final analysis, other nations will not be able to answer our distress signals as they too, will be preoccupied with maintaining themselves due to their own storms. Some of their storms will be weather related, but many will be related to famine, disease and war.

Stronger nations that have a hunger for war will engage in such, attacking the weaker with vengeance. Happy will they be for the opportunity to wage war without concern for the mighty Eagle Nation who is now floundering in a sea of destruction caused by severe weather, earthquakes, fire, volcanoes, disease and political and economic failure.

I was additionally told that we, mankind, have polluted our Earth so badly, that she will have to bathe herself to get rid of the filth. She will wash the land clean to make it fresh and new; hence, the rains. And so, just as the Earth will protect herself, we too, must take steps to protect ourselves.

Upon such a warning, wisdom dictates that we would be foolish not to put food away for those rainy days which lay ahead; especially the grains. The land upon which we have always depended will have little usable space for growing large quantities of any kind of food. This Earth is no longer concerned for the welfare of her inhabitants. She is concerned for herself, her own existence, her very survival.

She is alive.

In addition, I have been told that the waters will act as a lubricating agent to ease her "cracks."

At first, I did not understand what my unseen friends were trying to tell me; but, I have now been told the water will help lubricate the cracks (faults) where necessary slippage will take place. This lubricating effect will help prevent the land from rupturing herself too badly, and will ease the intensity of her shaking (earthquakes).

Going further into the dream, leaving behind the discussion of grain and rain, etc., finds us looking at the issue of Stone Mountain and the Stone Tablet.

I have the distinct feeling that we are looking at Stone Mountain since this Georgia mountain is solid granite, and it will be used by the people of that area when they seek temporary safety from the dramatically changing Earth; when the great waters come.

The rest of this dream deals with the Stone Tablets that were representatives of two hills; each identified by large protruding rocks. These rocks can be located somewhere near Stone Mountain. Within these rocks, or within the hills themselves, can be found information showing that these floods have occurred before. This type of change (current, predicted Earth changes) has been experienced by man, in this country, before. The proof lies within those hills and is "chiseled in stone."

The pebble/ruby is symbolic of valuable information which has previously been discarded by someone, or more accurately, several someones. The information was considered to be of very little value; it was just another "pebble" among the many; of minimal value; simply not worth keeping.

The key here, is that an old geological discovery thought to be of little value, has been discarded.

Let me explain more specifically: Around the area of Stone Mountain there are two hills of meaningful value (the ruby). On these hills are two monoliths which are points of identification. Within the hills, or the monoliths themselves, can be found scientific/archeological information of significant value to humankind in preparation for the forthcoming Earth changes.

The scientific community has already examined similar information or even this particular area itself. They see the information as meaningful (the ruby) but not meaningful enough to be kept and presented to the people. The information *was* briefly saved from the trash can by being set aside for further scrutiny (ruby placed on the wall beside trash can), but eventually met its demise like so many other pieces of data. It was considered just one more piece of already known information and not worth keeping.

This should not have been the case!

My friends tell me this data has been recorded by time and circumstance for us to use now. The information will also bring us knowledge as to the people who once inhabited that particular segment of land long ago; a time period unknown to current thinking.

If scientists would be more persistent, push their curiosity to the brink, they would find information which is "set in stone" (the stone tablet). The historic information found there, has been carefully recorded (chiseled) in the stone and we have been told where to find it.

Our current scientific documentation concerning Mother Earth and her previous peoples is seriously deficient. My unseen friends tell me that we do not give proper credit to the actual age of both her and her inhabitants.

I am also aware, through my unseen friends, that many in the more curious segment of our scientific community have already discovered or rediscovered) this "ruby" and have been excited with the "new" information. They have presented their findings to their professors and colleagues stating various possibilities and probabilities only to discover that they cannot get their "findings" published.

I do not know exactly why.

My unseen friends tell me that there is a "force of hindrance" involved.

That is all I know.

My telepathic and dream teachers have instructed me that humans do not properly examine a piece of evidence. We tend to relate everything to our knowns, and if it does not match what we have been taught, we discount the evidence as worthless. I am told that our approach is wrong; it is backwards. We need to reverse our thinking. We need to "back into" the information we are seeking in order to find the beginning.

These Earth changes which are about to occur have all occurred before. Evidence of these changes has been well documented. Whether the documentation lies in layers of soil, is ground in stone, or is somehow recorded by a past civilization, is really not important. The importance is, that material already found could substantiate our long, lost past and be a message of hope to the people of this America during these frightening times ahead.

And so it is, that being provided with the above information from my telepathic friends, I wonder "why" we must contend with a "force of hindrance" in our search for truth from the past?

Who is hiding the keys to our ancient history and why?

Chapter 6

PERSISTENT TEACHERS

Still at my parents' home in Maryland, I find myself awakening to the constant complaining of my father's feathered friend, Knuckle Head. I know this Mocking Bird is perched somewhere among the dark green foliage of the wide-leafed Norway maple just outside my open window.

Quietly reflecting on my situation, eyes still closed, I realize that I have been allowed to awaken; to rest from the onslaught on dreams just witnessed.

A cool morning breeze takes advantage of my open window to creep in silently and bring temporary relief to this body bathed in perspiration. The locusts have begun their traditional singing; a warning to all who listen that today will be another hot, muggy day so typical of the East Coast.

My hands and arms reach out across the flowered, percale bed sheets in search of cooler areas only to find that all have yielded to summer's humidity and become damp in areas where I have not yet lain.

Attempting to clear my head from all remnants of sleep, I desperately try to sense, from drifting conversations, who is doing what. The children at least sound happy.

I push myself up into a seated position on the edge of the tweed-covered hide-a-bed that has been cradling my torso in the spare room. My mind still reeling from the adventurous avenues I have just explored, my brother's cat wanders into the room and howls profusely, letting me know that I am the last of the humans to rise.

Head still groggy, I gently pick up the cat and slowly meander into the living room, where cheerful voices seem the loudest. I am greeted warmly by all, except my mother, who suggests a cup of coffee... since I look so terrible.

Staggering into the kitchen in search of the fresh brew, I had to admit, I felt drugged.

With coffee now in hand, I re-enter the living room to discuss plans for the day. Mom and the children said they were going swimming; did I care to join them?

I tried to make my "yes" sound exuberant, but it did not pass the listening ears of a loving mother.

"Why don't you just go back to bed?" she laughed. "We'll see you later."

I'm glad she sees the humor in all of this, but as for me, humor is non-existent. I have never felt so "drugged" in an awakened state in all my life.

Finishing my coffee and stumbling back to the spare room, it has become quite apparent that my unseen friends were not finished with my lessons for the day. As I climb into bed for another enforced sleep state, I begin wondering how many of these crash courses I will have to take. This is getting tedious, and my brain is reaching its saturation point.

Sleepily, I contemplate the persistence of my teachers from another world as I feel around for my favorite pillow. Securing it comfortably under my head, sleep rapidly overtakes me and I am whisked away for another message.

This time, I am walking up a steep, dirt road that winds along the edge of a grassy foot hill. My dream interpreter is with me.

DREAM... **He is accompanying me to the top of this hill where I know a tower to be. This tower is our destination, and it is essential for me to reach the top; not him.**

We are stopped by what appears to be a police officer from the city below who informs us our lives are in danger if we continue our journey. My senses immediately alert me to the fact that this officer belongs to a group known only as "the Frightening Force" which has suddenly taken over our land, but he does not truly wish to be a part of it. We are allowed to run back down the hill towards the city.

As I run, my ears are picking up a sound that is far more high-pitched then the pounding of my heart. It's beginning to hurt my ear drums. I know it has to do with the Frightening Force, but I don't know what it is.

Breathing heavily as we reach the bottom of the hill, my dream interrupter is telling me that I must enter the city alone. It is I who must see, feel and experience what is

taking place. I need to personally encounter what is happening to this nation in far more detail then my current understanding.

Taking a deep breath and moving forward, I enter what I know to be my own neighborhood and immediately perceive a terrifying sense of dread. My heart is beating even more rapidly than before. I can't say I like my assignment; I wish my companion would come with me.

Taking another deep breath, I look around and determine this neighborhood to be from the not-too-distant future. It's really eerie and I intuitively sense that all the people have turned against one another; not openly, but behind one another's backs. No adults are permitted to travel, even a block, without obtaining special permission. No child can be trusted; parents fear their own offspring.

The scene has now changed and I find myself seated in the living room of my own home. I sense that other family members are elsewhere within this same abode as my attention is quickly drawn to an adult woman who works in my house.

Her services have long been appreciated and she is someone I have always trusted. But now, she has become a willing participant in the actions of this Hideous Force that grips the nation.

After so many years of working for us her job now is to watch every move we make and report our activities. I know I cannot release her from employment because that would be a dead give-away to my knowledge of, and opposition to, this Frightening Force.

I must be careful in what I say and do. I know that she will "turn me in" if in any way I attempt to leave this house or circumvent the New Order of things, but I have to try. I have a feeling that the situation is only going to get worse and I cannot continue to live like this. Love, joy, freedom and trust are things of the past. I quickly devise a plan of escape.

Purposely distracting this paid employee, I give her the task of sewing a button on a shirt. I know the job will not take long and my absence will soon be discovered; I must hurry.

As I leave the house, slipping quietly through the front door, I wonder what caused this woman to become a volunteer in the works of this Frightening Force; but, I cannot afford to worry about her now; I must be "outside" to see what is going on.

Casually jogging down the street, not knowing what I will fall victim to, my heart races in fear. I know the rules one must follow in this New Order of things and I am violating one of them: adults are not allowed to roam the streets; they must have special permission... and have none.

It is daylight, but I fail to see any adults outside, or even a reflection of one in the housing windows. They're in hiding; not surprising. There are no automobiles, no beautiful flower gardens, no song birds, no pets to be seen anywhere. The silence is deafening.

The lawns and streets are immaculate; pitifully clean, as though the essence of life has been squeezed out of every living thing. I have no idea who takes care of them. I believe this new world is "chemically treated"; there isn't an insect around; all appears artificial.

The houses are neat and tidy; painted white, with no evidence of needed repairs. I cannot see into the backyards... the houses are too tightly jammed together.

I sense the children of this era are the well-planned and carefully manipulated creation of long-time planning by those who wish to rule. It seems as though this force has convinced these young minds that most adults can be, and should be, subdued. I don't understand how they did that without entrapping themselves, but it has been accomplished.

Any adult (not a member of the Frightening Force) who does not comply with the wishes of the reigning powers will be "turned in" by the labor force, who for the most part, seem to be the children (or adults with child-like minds).

Still jogging down the street, I see two children off in the distance; a boy and a girl. One is riding a bicycle, the other a tricycle. They are heading towards me.

As they approach, I am aghast! They are unlike any children I have ever seen. All seems normal, except their eyes. These seemingly hollow eyes are wide open, but contain nothing more then deep, black voids. It's as though "nobody's home." They appear to be in a trance; their young bodies mere shells with no soul inside. I cannot grasp how we lost control of our environment, our freedoms and our children.

I know these children will "turn me in" to the Frightening Force if I do not come up with a good excuse for being out of my house.

While contemplating my next move, I see a man poorly disguised as Santa Claus moving ever closer towards me. He is on a bicycle, but still some distance away. I realize that he is coming to see me and I must make contact with him; I must pass these children without causing suspicion.

I begin waving a small piece of paper in front of the two children, pretending it is an official pass, while chanting in a sassy, sing-song fashion, "I got special permission."

Seeing my predicament, my would-be friend cries out, "Ho-Ho-Ho" in a typical Santa Claus style. This is done in an attempt to curtail any curiosity which might arise from the children over the piece of paper I am waving. It seems to be working.

As his bicycle approaches me he loudly shouts, so the children can hear, "Want any Top Value Stamps?"

I'm confused! I have no idea what he is talking about, but suddenly realize that he is discretely trying to hand me something.

I reply in the affirmative, extending my arm so that fingers can clasp what is being given.

Quickly scanning these "stamps," I observe that they are fake and actually of writing paper quality. Turning them over, I find a message handwritten in crayon on the back. The message is faintly written making it difficult to read, but it does say something about teaching me a new song to sing.

This new song will be unlike the religious-style songs I have been accustomed to singing in the past. (I don't understand, but read on.)

The note further states that he "will convert me." I assume he means to his way of song. I am further told that this song is to be sung in a tower, and I believe it is at the top of the hill I was previously climbing when stopped by the police officer.

The note also informs me that the message of this new song is what the people will need to hear in order to help them destroy the ugly force which grips the land.

As I finish reading, I am still puzzled over everything taking place. Quickly glancing around, I find the children I encountered earlier now gone.

Once again, an awareness strikes me indicating that I must take immediate evasive action. I am told to obliterate this written message before the dreaded force gets a hold of it.

Have the children reported me to those in charge?

Heart pounding, I nonchalantly tear it into little pieces as I walk off the street, keeping the pieces firmly within my grip. My plans are to throw the tiny pieces into numerous trash cans where they will be covered with other trash and undiscoverable.

My ears are beginning to ring. I've heard this sound before. I hold my breath and listen intently to be certain; then I know. The Frightening Force is coming.

Quickly, I hurdle a chain-link fence in order to throw some pieces of the message into a nearby trash can.

Lifting the lid, I am frantic to see that the can has recently been emptied. It will now be so easy for this force to go through can by can and piece the message together.

I am obsessed with uncontrollable fear me as I realize the Force is almost upon me. I know that the man posing as "Santa Claus" has been unable to escape; he has been arrested; he will go to prison. I know too, that if I am

**caught with this message still in my possession, it will be
used as evidence against the Santa and me.**
I don't know what to do!
Shall I just swallow the message?
**Quivering, and near tears, I tightly hold my ears and
close my eyes as the ringing rocks my head.**
The Frightening Force is almost on me!

I can no longer stand the fright and awaken in great horror. Not
being totally awake, I can not fathom what Santa Claus and Top Value
stamps have to do with the message at all, but clearly understand that I
will be taught "**a new song to sing.**"

Now more alert, I am told the main objective of the dream is to
show conditions that currently exist within our nation and provide us
with a better understanding of just how "controlled" we have become.

I am also told that the people of this nation want to "come out of
hiding." They want to gain better control. They seek truth; truth on all
fronts.

My dream companion explains further that people are awaiting this
"**new song**" that I am to sing. This new "song" will be imperative for all
people to "hear" in order to crush the miserable force that holds this
nation in a vice grip.

I am told not to fear my audience; however, I am forewarned that in
singing this new song, I will put my life at risk.

This is clear!

The Santa Claus was not actually "arrested" and thrown into
"prison." These two words are symbolic.

"Arrested" in this case refers to something which is being
"subdued" or "held under control" while the term "prison" represents
something which is "put away" or "buried deep" (entombed).

When we think of the character of this jolly symbolism of
Christmas, we might well create a long list of emotions that stir within
us; cheer, renewed hope, goodwill, happiness, faithfulness, honesty, etc.;
but, he may well be considered "the Spirit of Christmas" or, simply put:
"Breathe of Joy." But in the final analysis, we could all agree that he
would never lie; he would always speak truth, bringing great joy to all he
contacts.

51

This particular Santa costume was a little ragged and didn't fit too well. It was described as leaving the individual "poorly disguised." The poor disguise has two meanings.

My dream interrupter tells me this Santa's tattered costume represents "poorly disguised" truth and joy. It is telling us that the "truth" and "joy/goodwill" messages we hear from our leaders (both religious and political) are inaccurate; we are not getting the whole truth.

We are fed both misinformation and disinformation; we are misled for the purpose of guiding our thinking along the avenues of governed conclusions. When the Frightening Force wishes to have the people back their pre-planned moves, before it takes action, it will provide the people with a story, in the hopes of winning approval. These stories are carefully calculated to support their ultimate goals; nothing more. But, by following this pattern of pre-determined existence, we are slowly losing our freedoms; true joy.

My unseen friends are telling us that our truth is being "arrested" (being brought to a stop; being kept in custody by authority of law; being withheld from view by the unsuspecting peoples of this land).

In the dream, I knew that Santa would be taken to "prison" which was to further exemplify the withholding, or confinement of information from the Americans; truth, and sincere joy being buried deep.

The second meaning to the Santa Claus costume is to represent a disguise that would allow everyone who sees him to feel comfortable. He is familiar. He does not pose a threat. The children readily accepted him and let him pass even though he was an adult; an adult that they were taught to mistrust. The costume provided him with the mechanism necessary to bring assistance to the whole community (mankind) without creating undue suspicion.

This Santa also represents the Forces of Good and is illustrating that it will be necessary to "ride through" (Santa riding the bicycle) this coming nightmare.

We, in turn, will have to "modify" or "disguise" our appearance (again, the Santa Claus suit), as well as our words to produce a comfort level within the individuals who, for whatever reason, support the Frightening Force. It is hoped that by becoming one with them, and speaking a language they understand, some might be saved that would have been, otherwise, lost to the Dark Forces.

My telepathic communicators state it another way; its like going under cover. If we are to appeal to the youth of this nation, we must become like the youth, seek their comfort level. Not that we are to absorb the negative aspects of this youth, but merely become one with them in a manner that allows us to penetrate their confidence in order to deliver the message and bring to them the truth of their existence.

If we are to speak to the weak and afflicted, then we must appear to be weak and afflicted, not that we really are, only that we seem that way in order to win their confidence in order to deliver the message to their understanding.

Again, it works in the same fashion for the rich or poor, those inside and outside the law, etc., in order to save as many as possible, we are to disguise ourselves so that we appear to be one with them; to become like them. They will listen to the message from one of their own kind, but they mistrust the words of those unlike themselves.

It should be noted here, that we are clearly told not to by-pass or go around the situation, we are to "ride through." My unseen friends fully expect that ALL who wish to be freed from the Frightening Force will participate in getting the message out once they hear it from the tower. So as I "sing" the new song, they can then choose to **"hear or not to hear"**; free themselves or continue to live in bondage.

Some people may not be familiar with Top Value stamps; please let me explain.

Some years ago, along the east coast of the United States, these stamps were used in the same manner as S&H Green Stamps, and other worthy stamps given as tokens of appreciation and goodwill throughout numerous grocery stores. They were an enticement to continue shopping at that particular store.

Once collected, they were glued in specifically provided books, or on paper sheets, to be held until needed to participate in one of the company's exchange programs. The exchange program offered a variety of items in which you could then use your stamps to "purchase" other consumable products either edible or non-edible.

I, personally, used several of these stamp programs over the years and appreciated the opportunity to stretch my purchasing power.

However, in the dream scenario, my unseen friends are asking us to look at things a little differently.

The Top Value stamps in this case, represent a ploy to maintain a bribed loyalty; a carefully devised tactic to influence your judgment.

The stamps, when turned over, lacked glue and were therefore, useless (had no value) even though they were being handed to me (presented to the people) as Top Value.

This has nothing whatsoever to do with the promotion of stamps for the benefit of tokens of appreciation by various stores. This dream illustration applies to programs which are promoted to the unsuspecting public as "Top Value."

We, the people, are faithfully spending our hard-earned dollars to support an entity who is providing enticements as a ploy to hold on to our loyalty. This entity is our government and its favored few. Many of the "stamps" have no value.

If we were to more closely examine items being billed as Top Value (or even worse yet, look at the ones we never knew about), we would find that all too many never were meant to benefit the people in the long run.

So... these stamps, having no value, are seen as being scrap paper and a message is hurriedly written in crayon on them with the awareness that once read, it must be thrown away.

Writing in crayon indicates childishness, being juvenile or immature. It does not portend that this Santa is childish but rather, points to the fact that the message will be delivered to an audience that has not been allowed to fully develop.

We are that audience from which truth has been articulately hidden. The problem is, very few of us even recognize its absence.

In addition, my dream companion explains that the message was never meant to be physically destroyed. It was meant to be "swallowed" by me (or held) until that time in which I was further instructed to publish my first book. This information was not to be tossed out (thrown in a trash can) to others who could not appreciate its value. It was to be "stomached" until further notice.

Notice has now been given.

Not all the people living in this New Order will be so easily controlled by the long-existing Dark Force that is beginning to dominate our land. Even some of those who are sworn to uphold the wrongdoings of the force will quietly help those who oppose it. The only reason they will align themselves with the force is to save themselves, their families, and to help as many people as they can.

Now is the time to be very guarded in what you say and do. Choose your confidants wisely.

These are times of great sorrow when brother will turn against brother, son against father, daughter against mother, and so forth. We are told not to trust a neighbor and do not bestow confidence in a friend. We are told to speak with caution, weighing each word carefully and watch the children. Children will rise up against their parents, bring about false witness, and have them put to death.

I was later told that the high-pitched frequency that bothered my ears was a controlling frequency being used today. I was given the word "electromagnetic" but do not know how this applies to what The Advocate was telling me. He explained that the youth of our land will be much more receptive to it; they will be totally unaware of what is happening to them; hence, the hollowed-eyed children. Animals too, will be negatively affected by this event.

In addition, I was later shown three electrical waves with a "rider" attached and cannot be certain whether this wave provided the above problem or is an entirely different set of circumstances of which we need to be concerned. I was told that the frequency of this carrier wave would change from time to time causing much sickness, both physically and mentally.

This is what my unseen companion showed me in a vision.

VISION... **I am watching a group of three electrical waves traveling though the air. They wave gracefully as they follow a specified course. One electrical wave causes me to examine it more closely as it does not appear as smooth as the other two.**

Upon minute scrutiny, I clearly see a tiny black figure attached to this wave. It is so thin, it looks like an animated "stick" figure. The eyes of the creature are exceptionally large for his otherwise small body. The creature is holding on to the electrical wave like a jockey riding in a horse race. However, unlike a jockey, his body and head are undulating in the same rhythm sequence as the electrical wave on which it is riding.

The tiny manifestation briefly looks at me with its beady eyes, then quickly turns its gaze forward. In an

55

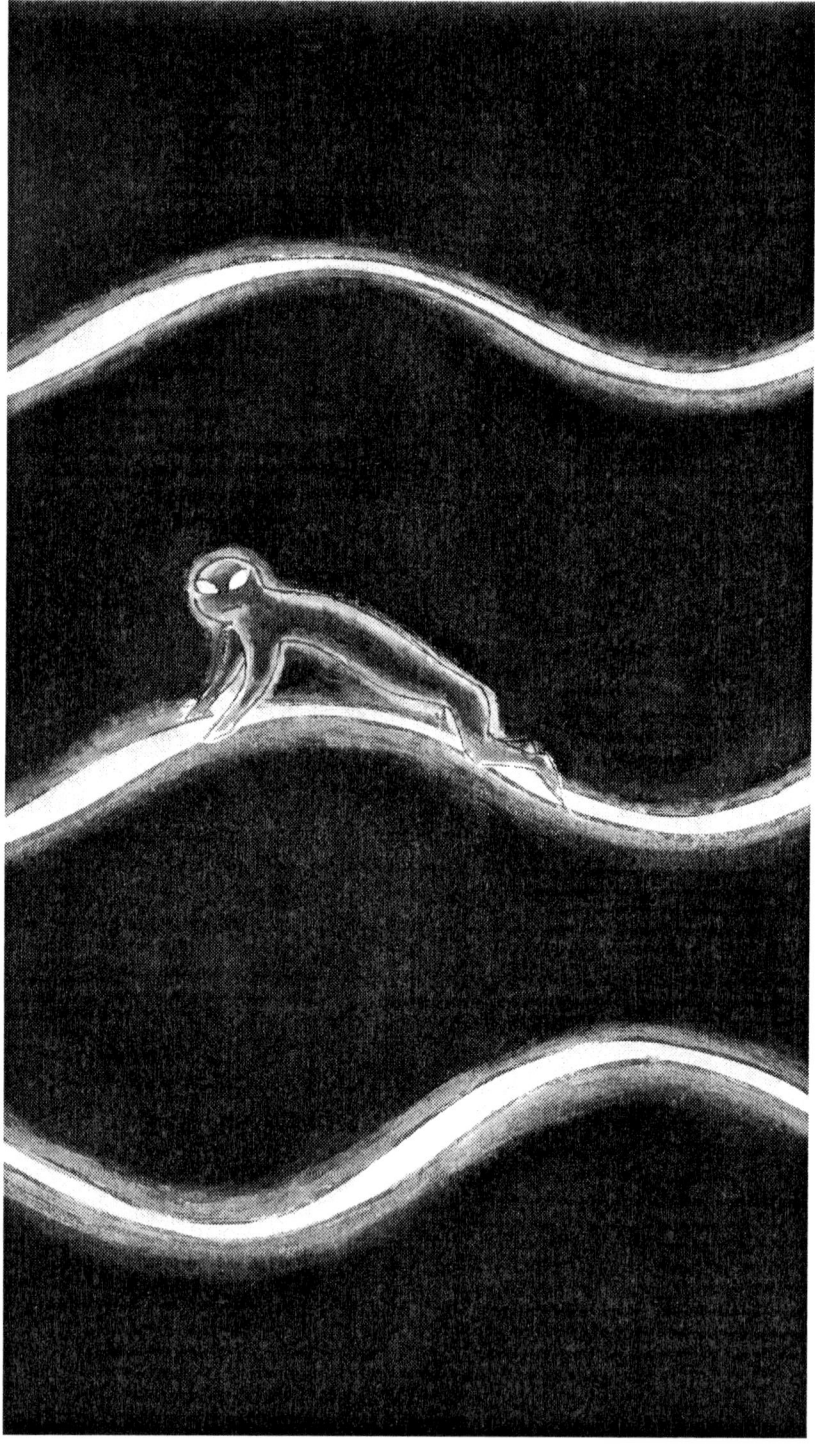

attempt to hide from my view, it buries its face into the back of the electrical wave upon which it is riding. It does not seem to mind my presence, but would have preferred not to have been discovered.

One might say that this "jockey" (or rider) is holding on in "piggyback" fashion. It enters our buildings by attaching itself to another frequency; riding on the back of another wave (piggy-back).

Because the rider's color was black, he will bring with him much sickness. Often, the created sicknesses that are related to this rider are far greater than mere flu-like symptoms. I sense this jockey has a specific destination when he arrives in our homes; that is, he is sent to target a specific area of our bodies. Some affected people will find difficulty with internal organs such as gallbladder, kidneys, spleen, appendix; others, the mind.

It means that your health is being bombarded with negative particles being carried in on electrical circuitry which are vibrating at a specified frequency to purposely harm your organs.

You are being programmed to be ill!

Chapter 7

BEYOND WHERE BIRDS FLY

Escaping from the dream world of a tower, Santa Claus and hollow-eyed children, I am slowly throwing off the remnants of sleep through the sounds of splashing water coming from my mother's pool. With a wee bit of enthusiasm, I venture toward the kitchen for more coffee, and glance at the clock. It is two o'clock in the afternoon! I have spent half the day in bed!

Still in a daze, and bewildered by the amount of time that has elapsed, I join everyone at the pool. Mom greeted me warmly and said something to the effect that, "the dead has risen."

What a sense of humor!

I did know, however, that she was only teasing since I had previously told her about the dream siege and what was taking place.

Mom understood and supported me one hundred percent; she has from the very beginning. I also knew she would be anxious to know more about what I had seen; however, relaying the dreams would have to wait until tomorrow since I wanted to spend some time with the children and much of the day had already vanished.

That night I found myself still tired even though I had "slept all day." I laid in my bed listening to the night sounds which provided a welcomed lullaby. I heard a night bird of some sort singing and my mind questioned, "Shouldn't he be sleeping? Shouldn't he be...?"

I fell asleep with the sensation of floating.

DREAM... **I am floating. I am comfortable. I do not see anything, but sense that I am floating. My eyes are closed.**

Suddenly my body experiences great acceleration and startled, I open my eyes to see that we are traveling at a great speed _away from the Earth_. VERY high above the

59

Earth. I am not happy at this! I do not like great heights or speeds!

Then a calmness prevails. The height no longer bothers me. We are no longer moving. We are stationary. I am surrounded by something that causes me to feel secure and looking out of what I believe to be a window. I am directed to look down.

Startled, I hear myself say, "Oh!" as I find myself positioned in a north by northwest direction looking at the western portion of the United States. I think I am actually stationed somewhere over Mexico.

It's so difficult to tell; the land all runs together in harmony; not broken up like the detailing on maps. It certainly is different. I can't tell where one state ends and another begins.

I see the Pacific Ocean, but know I am not supposed to focus on the water. I am supposed to watch the land; very specifically, the western portion of California.

I observe that California is brown in color, but I do not understand the significance of the color.

Shouldn't California be a pretty green? This seems unimportant.

Suddenly, a crack appears on the land and once again I hear myself say, "Oh," as I watch a long, jagged, somewhat vertical crack develop rapidly; as easily as a fabric tear.

The crack begins just above a hump on the northern shore of California and proceeds to somewhere just south of Los Angeles.

As I am studying the features of the land, to get a better look at the southern area traversed by the crack, the land on the western portion of the crack begins to slip into the ocean. It does not appear that the land falls away; it just slides, steadily downward into the ocean.

As I try to absorb what I am seeing, my unseen companions determine I have seen enough here and whisk me away again. This time we head east.

I find myself moving so rapidly that I cannot see anything except a blurry brownish something below me.

I am sure that it is still the Earth, and very specifically the extreme southern portion of the United States.

Not being too happy with this great speed, I once again close my eyes with the certainty that we are going to crash.

Due to a rapid shift in pressure on new places in my body, I suddenly open my eyes to see what is happening. Much to my dismay, I find that we are plummeting towards the Atlantic Ocean at an outlandish speed! I feel we are going much too fast and hate the awful feeling in my stomach; however, I am entirely too frightened to complain. I just grimace and hold my breath.

Now, holding my breath is not too tough because the speed at which we are descending produces enough pressure on my intestines, stomach and chest that breathing is difficult at best. Oh, how I dislike speed!

Bracing myself for a hit on the water, we suddenly halt in mid-air as a HUGE gray object covered in barnacles arises abruptly from the sea, displacing an enormous amount of water. "A whale!" I gasp in horror and clamber frantically backward to get out of its reach.

But before the words are even out of my mouth, I understand that this is not a whale at all! This is land; old land! I instinctively know we have long awaited its arrival.

Upon rising the following morning, I asked Mom for her Road Atlas in order to get a better look at the California coastline. Having found the book, I flipped through the pages to the one marked "California" and first looked at the northern end of the state where I had watched the crack develop. I found that area to be around a town known as Eureka.

With my finger, I traced the line as best I remembered it, all the way down to somewhere just below Los Angeles. I could not pinpoint the southern most tip due to my space traveling friends taking me away from the coastal region before I had a good chance to look at it.

I suspect that much of my inability to locate the fault's southern tip may well have to do with inexperience on my part; I was too slow in my observations.

I never did see the entire land mass completely inundated by water. I guess this was not an important issue to those who were showing me this future event. In any case, my traveling companions removed me from that area at a moment in time when I could no longer witness what was about to take place.

From my perch, high above the Earth, I only saw it crack and slowly slip, straight down, into the mighty sea. I knew, however, that the western most portion of the land had been claimed by the sea, and that now a new coastline existed.

I also came to know the reason that California was depicted as being brown in color. It was to illustrate one of two conditions: rain or drought.

Since my position in the sky was located somewhere in Mexico, I am quite sure I was skimming across the extreme southern portion of the United States and over the state of Florida, when we dipped into the Atlantic Ocean. All of these areas were brown too, as I viewed them from my north facing position. This would include the states of Arizona, New Mexico, Texas, Louisiana, Mississippi, Alabama, Florida and Georgia. I suspect the entire "brown" picture was due to an enormous amount of water; flooding.

The land that appeared as a "**whale**," was somewhere off the coast of the Georgia/Florida border or perhaps even a little more South. I was actually under the impression that it may well cover that entire region.

It was no small piece of land!

I was so startled by the massive object and so close to the ocean that I failed to note my exact location in relationship to some recognizable eastern coastline. However, I felt certain that it would rise off the coasts of these two southeastern states and extend beyond the tip of Florida.

Having explained all of the above to Mom, she promptly asked me, "Have you ever read Edgar Cayce?"

I had no idea who Edgar Cayce was and gave every indication of this in my reply.

"What does he have to do with what I just told you?" I asked in surprise.

Mom said that she had read something about land rising off the coast of Bimini in one of Edgar Cayce's books. I had no idea where in the world Bimini was, but had to conclude that it must be somewhere off the lower southeastern portion of the United States in order to coincide with my recent adventure.

And so, with these words Mom introduced me to Edgar Cayce; a quiet man of simple taste, who was devoted to his Creator and his fellow man. The book that Mom loaned me to read was entitled, EDGAR CAYCE - THE SLEEPING PROPHET.

Having now read about the man, I find him utterly fascinating. However, at this point in my life, not entirely believable. The part I have a hard time dealing with is reincarnation.

I find it interesting that he too, was a Presbyterian, just like me. It is also nice to know that another human being knew about the rising land mass in the Atlantic.

I now have solid confirmation on my "**whale**" sighting.

Chapter 8

MANY ROOMS

The return to our home in Atlanta brought new excitement for both me and the children. We now had an audience of friends and neighbors for our tales of adventure. But, I told my new dreams only to my husband for I dared not mention them to anyone else in our neighborhood. I had no idea how people might react to such matters and cared not to be ostracized from my own community.

The tale of the mysterious doctor, however, could easily be told. Most people viewed it as a lucky coincidence and saw nothing miraculous at all. Those who did see the event as miraculous discussed the matter quietly among themselves.

I was glad to enter the land of dreams from my own bed again, although my dreams were not as vivid and as easy to recall as they had been at my parents' house.

Perhaps, this was due to my preoccupations with being wife, mother, and keeper of the house and gardens.

The dreams persisted and one night a dream began by taking me on a puzzling journey that continued for three whole nights; something like a TV mini-series.

DREAM... The first night found me going from room to room, in various buildings, where conversations with my parents' friends, some old school chums and a few relatives were very brief. I knew the conversations were of minor importance, but was unclear as to what I should focus on.

At the beginning of the second night of this dream, I was given a quick review of the previous night's episode. Having quickly digested the previous night's information, I was introduced to the current evening's issues and proceeded with the lessons.

65

I was directed to enter a tiny upstairs room whose access was obtained by climbing a ladder centrally located within that room.

Upon arrival, I found my husband, Johnny, seated on a wooden bench that lined the wall on one side of the room. Sitting was necessary as an extraordinarily low ceiling made standing impossible.

We sat uncomfortably avoiding a possible fall through the large entrance hole in the floor.

At a certain point in our conversation I was encouraged by my dream companion to leave the room by means of a door located immediately to my left, which necessitated my climbing over my husband to reach it.

Unfortunately, in the process of climbing across my husband's lap, I woke up before I could see what was on the other side of that door.

On the third night, I fell asleep wondering what the inside of the other room looked like. I have no idea why I even thought that, but immediately found myself in a great, stately, elegant dining hall fit for a king.

I walked around this room in awe, touched the magnificent, highly polished walls of rare woods, and stood gazing with delight at the many other fine woods used in creating this luxurious room.

At the termination of this particular episode I was given two words, "many mansions."

In review of my mini-series, the first night had taken me into a large, immaculately clean, white barn with an indoor roof line that must have been at least three stories high.

No animals had been seen.

I had then proceeded to other, seemly insignificant buildings and then on to the main house where I was taken to a bedroom. Here, the main topic of conversation had been antique dolls.

The second night had taken me to a tiny room where my husband was the only other occupant, and on the third night I found myself staring in awe at the beautifully polished walls, floors and furniture of a magnificent dining hall seemingly destined for royalty.

I had no clue as to what my dream companion was trying to tell me. The only "quick" response my mind could conjure up was an immediate connection to a biblical passage in which it is reported that the Christ had stated: "In my Father's house are many mansions."

Night after night went by without further instruction. I stayed alert for my companions's messages, but perhaps, too alert. I was like a child first starting kindergarten: so much was new and I wanted to know everything.

I soon learned that when time was spent concentrating on these matters from afar, they eluded me. I found that when I was too focused with the physical eyes and ears of my human form, I lacked the freedom to see and hear from sources well beyond the boundaries of this earthly plane we call home.

It was, indeed, a vast learning experience. Time gave me to know that only in the moments of a relaxed mind and body, or in my time of great need, did the words and dreams come to produce a lesson, message, or words of comfort.

One source of peaceful moments was gardening, so I decided that a stint of weeding was long overdue. With small tools in hand, I tackled intruders that were crowding out the grasses of my backyard.

I carefully staked out my area of attack, forming a small square by placing a stick in each corner and running a string from stake to stake. My plan was to complete the weeding in one area and then move two stakes to form another square. Thus, I would deal with the weeds in little squares all around the backyard.

Satisfied with my newly formed playpen, I ran back into the house to get our guinea pig for company. Pig, as we called her, was very fond of eating grass and enjoyed human companionship. Once settled within my handmade cage, I began to rescue the grasses from a villainous clutch.

Having pulled and prodded many a weed, I wiped the sweat from my face, shifted my position on the turf, and sat down, stroking the guinea pig in a mindless manner.

I considered the nature of weeds.

Surely, God does not put all these weeds in the grasses of man's home just to frustrate him. They *must* have a useful purpose that has escaped our present recognition. Because they are so abundant, and thrive so well in all kinds of soil, they must have served both man and beast in some distant past.

Further research would be needed.

I returned to pulling weeds, but without the certainty that these flourishing plants were actually the villains I once thought them to be.

As I continued to await lessons from the Great Beyond, my exploration into weeds had some exciting results; many were edible. I now questioned the sanity of man in throwing away perfectly good food that grew in his backyard without cultivation. Of course, he would have to forage; not an activity easily accepted in modern suburbia.

I learned that we had abandoned the use of edible weeds when grocery stores became accessible. Housewives were encouraged to save time and provide nutritious foods for their families; so we all jumped in and supported our local grocer, leaving behind the age-old knowledge on how to provide for ourselves; how to be self-sufficient.

We quickly became totally dependent on this new found supplier of assorted foods from every part of the world. In addition, by nature of this new merchandizing technique, we need to only shop at one market, and happily participate in a wonderful taste-testing frenzy.

I suspected that the American Indians and people living in certain parts of the Rocky Mountains and Appalachians were still familiar with the use of these persistent greens; but, middle and upper class America would look away in disdain.

How sad.

How wasteful of time, money and *free* nutritional renderings!

At the dinner table one night, our teenager spoke of a recent cross-country practice run in which he, along with a number of the other participants grabbed as many muscadines as possible when running past a certain point. He said that these grapes provided enough moisture to keep them going. They also provided the runners with a little sugar for energy.

I inquired further concerning these wild grapes and was told that they hung virtually everywhere. So, I asked David to bring one or two home that I might examine them in order to identify these tasty morsels in the wild.

He did as I asked and I examined them carefully.

Now with a clear picture in mind, having seen these grapes, I headed out to find them in our surrounding woods. In addition, I had just finished reading Euell Gibbons' STALKING THE WILD ASPARAGUS and was anxious to see what else I could find.

I ventured out more and more frequently to "stalk" the wild edibles, and began tossing a few of these goodies into the summer salads. Dandelion leaves sprinkled with violets and nasturtiums were too much for my children to cope with.

The family response was polite, but firm rejection. Each would carefully scan his or her salad and selectively remove any unwanted intruders. I'm sure they all thought I had lost my good senses.

They were not alone.

I noticed that the neighbors, who once waved to me while I was on foraging expeditions, no longer even acknowledged my presence.

Previously, automobile horns had honked and occupants waved enthusiastically in a gesture of greeting. Now, the horns were silent and the occupants pretended not to see me. My oldest son commented that I was embarrassing the neighbors, although I was pleased to note that he did not indicate I was embarrassing him, also.

I should have known. We belonged to upper-middle class America and they didn't eat weeds and wild things.

Spring molded herself into summer and soon autumn was well underway. School was in session and I found the children in need of various items from the local bookstore. I considered more reading material for myself also, particularly in the realm of harvestable wild foods, or perhaps something more on Edgar Cayce. Books were my favorite passion, next to gardening.

As we wandered around the bookstore, each of us darting to our own particular area of interest, I found myself searching for... I had no idea what. I just became aware that I was most seriously searching. I felt I was looking for a special something that would jump out and say "buy me."

Suddenly, I realized that even though my physical eyes were still scanning the rows of book titles, my mind's eye had already found what it was looking for. My eyes darted back up a few rows and firmly fixed themselves on a book entitled "**MANY MANSIONS.**"

I could scarcely believe what I saw. These were that exact same words given to me by my dream companion. This book had actually been pre-selected for me. That's why he had shown me all those rooms and given me the two words "**many mansions**" some months ago.

The children had each found whatever they needed or wanted and approached me, treasures in hand, to see if I had found something for myself.

I replied, somewhat dumbfounded, "I think I'm supposed to buy that book," indicating which one by pointing to the shelf.

My oldest son tried to encourage me to purchase another book whose title I had mentioned quite often, but I said, with more conviction now, "No. I can't do that."

"I'm supposed to buy this one," I boldly stated, taking the book from the shelf and carrying my new found treasure to the cashier.

As it turned out, it was another story involving Edgar Cayce, but in addition, it gave me a wonderful insight into the true nature of reincarnation and the concept of karma. This was the very subject matter I had cowered from when reading the first book about Edgar Cayce that Mom had given me.

This new book carried me through the many rooms, the **"many mansions,"** the many dimensions of man's existence both in the material and spiritual world.

And so it was, that the very words that had haunted me for several months turned out to be the title to a book. My mysterious companion wanted me to learn about reincarnation and karma (the many rooms within my Father's house) and had therefore, not presented me with any new material until I had completed my first assignment.

How fascinating!

I didn't even know that I had been given an assignment!

The length of time that transpired from the end of that dream until I found the book on reincarnation was several months. I had been patiently waiting for my companion to speak of educated matters to me and could not understand why I was greeted with silence.

I found it quite interesting that no matter how long and intensely I had waited, watched and listened for my unseen friend to speak or take me on a walk through dreams again, he would not.

At the time, I could not understand why this was happening. Clearly, I reasoned, I had been given a command to write and record, but if he wasn't talking, how could I record?

During this period, great doubt had been creeping in and I found myself wondering if I was truly losing my mind or did all these things really take place. I still dared not say anything to anyone except Mom and my husband, and was becoming depressed and lonely.

Yes, actually lonely without the presence of my courtier. I could not understand why he had left me, or so I thought.

It had never occurred to me that he was waiting for *me* to do my part.

When I finally understood what was taking place, what my teacher was trying to accomplish, my heart and mind leaped with joy.

I was thrilled!

Karma and reincarnation, this revisited concept would take time to digest.

Well, time was something that I was not going to be allowed. I had found and read the prescribed book carefully, trying to digest the material without choking, and by doing this, completed some preliminary work in furthering my prescribed education. At this point, my unseen tutor felt the concept needed immediate attention.

Falling asleep one night, I found my mind to be on vacation with no concerns for the passing day, nor cares for a tomorrow that had yet to be born.

I thought this rather strange, as I normally picture myself on a hillside covered in wild flowers, where I overlook a beautiful meadow and soak up the smell of fresh pine needles; but not tonight. Suddenly, I found myself on a street in ancient Rome where throngs of people were shouting words of cheer.

DREAM... **I am a child of about 8 to 10 years of age. Very specifically, a child among many other children captured during a recent war. I don't know who my people are. I don't remember where I came from. This does not seem to matter.**

I cannot see very far ahead of me as the chariot I am walking behind blocks much of my view. I am greatly impressed by all the fanfare. Trumpets are blowing and the people of this great city are happily shouting as they stand in long rows along the sides of the streets.

The streets have some kind of leaves and palm fronds strewn on them. People of all ages are throwing flowers and flower petals.

I am immensely enjoying the celebration as I ceremoniously walk behind my captor's cart. I am not afraid of this soldier. He is very kind, gentle and seems so wise. I am pleased to be a part of this great parade which is, in part, to honor him.

The buildings are magnificent, nothing like where I came from. I sense that I came from a distant village, and that my people were predominantly farmers serving some other lord. But a different kind of lord, unlike these people of darker features.

The music, wide roads, beautiful white, shiny buildings, white, blue and purple robes worn by the people along the roadways give me a thrill. Many of their waists are encircled by gold sashes. Never have I encountered such splendor.

Another man is in the chariot with my soldier. This man drives the horses as my soldier holds on to the sides of the chariot, nodding his head ever so slightly in response to the throngs of people.

We children march first behind the chariot. We walk in ill-fashioned rows of five or six wide and about the same deep. Then come the women and young maidens. Last in the procession of slaves are the men; men of all ages. My soldier even keeps the old ones. He is kind to all.

Our parade passes by a stand where some women are being sold. I have to maintain a distance in my feelings for what is going on, especially for one of them. I recognize her. She is from my village.

They have stripped her naked and her current owner is pointing to various parts of her body with a long stick, pointing out her positive aspects. She is so sad. She hangs her head low in embarrassment, but the man with the stick keeps putting it under her chin to get her to lift her head up so that the beauty of her face can be seen by all.

I know she is married to one of our men and has a tiny baby. The baby is nowhere to be seen and I sense she will never see her baby or husband again.

Some of the men bidding on her are as dark as the bark on our trees and as black as coastal pebbles. Some are a golden brown; while the majority of them are wealthy men of this Roman race with light, golden skin.

Most of these Romans have dark hair. This too, is interesting to me as our hair and skin is so much lighter. My people are a little taller and more slender than these Romans, and our women are highly prized for their slender beauty and massive lengths of golden hair that dances with fire when the sun shines on it.

The parade scene has now disappeared and I find myself working at my master's villa. I am carrying water up a hill towards the main house. I am not allowed in the house. I do not serve there.

As I become aware of my own aging process, I am also aware of the life of my beloved soldier. Yes; I have fallen in love with my captor.

Being a slave girl, I know that it is impossible for me to ever marry him. I watch as he marries and divorces several times always harboring the thought that if he had been my husband I would have known how to treat him. I would have made him happy. I would have brought him peace. I feel that the other women just don't understand him; they are too concerned with their own personal pleasures.

I do not envy them for being married to him; however, I see them as poor examples of womanhood if he is always having to get rid of them. He is so beautiful; why can't they understand him.

Still in a semi-sleep state, I was left to understand that I lived out my life in this villa. I never married, or if I married, was so consumed by love for my captor that I paid little attention to the immediate life around me.

As I am thinking the above, a thought quickly takes form and brings my mind to a more awakened state. In sudden disbelief, I turn to look at my husband who is sound asleep beside me. With eyes wide, I stare at him.

I have just been told that the beautiful Roman soldier that I loved so many eons ago, and this man lying beside me, are one and the same. I am being told that the slave girl who wished to be married to her handsome Roman captor so many hundreds of years ago was actually married to him now.

My current husband, Johnny, was my beloved soldier from Rome.

I said nothing to anyone. I kept all these things to myself for a long time.

I laid awake for heaven knows how long. What I had just seen and been told was difficult to absorb. I simply could not.

I could only systematically try to process the information and store it in the recesses of my mind to pull out at a later date for further examination. But digest it at this time; never.

I was not entirely rejecting this new lesson, I merely chose to set it on a shelf where I could remove it for periodic review; thus, allowing my mind more time for contemplation.

Again, I was fighting with what my church had taught me, and I did not find that there was any room for the workings of karma and reincarnation.

As a child, my introduction to the word reincarnation was vague and had to do with the sacred cows of India. I had been told that the Asian Indians believed that once you died you came back as a cow. I never even knew whether this bore any truth or was some mischievous story.

Then along came a man by the name of Edgar Cayce who spoke of another form of reincarnation.

Too much was happening too fast.

I required time for mental processing!

My mind had a billion questions running through it. I was close to a brain circuit overload, and there was no one to talk to; no one with whom to share my thoughts, other than Mom and Johnny. But I just could not bring myself to even discuss with them what I had recently witnessed.

I found myself actually studying my husband. If I was to believe in karma, then what was I to complete with this man?

Was it his karma or mine?

In the karma described by Edgar Cayce, you are given the ability to work things out. These karmas may be in the form of something that you didn't get a chance to finish in a previous life, or you owe someone something or they owe you. Either way, one is granted the opportunity to set things straight in the hopes that these things do not have to occur again and again.

Forgiveness, total understanding, compassion are some of the ingredients of this thing known as karma.

I reasoned that perhaps this is what the Christ meant when he said that we should "turn the other cheek." If karma is a reoccurrence of happenings from the past, the only way to stop the continuous flow of a particular negative thought or deed is for someone to have total forgiveness; to turn the other cheek, so to speak. In this way, one is breaking the chain of negative events that had previously been set in perpetual motion; to cancel them entirely.

A shock wave hit me as I understood this present day match. I vaguely remember that my Roman soldier *did* love me, but due to his stature within the community could not marry me. I could have been his mistress, but never a wife.

I was much too proud to compromise.

I was now given the opportunity to prove to *myself* that I could be a better wife than all the other women he had been married to during those lovely days at the Roman villa. This was also his opportunity to marry the little slave girl who seemed so vivacious to him, and so naive.

I wondered how this would all play out, because at some point, the other women had to enter the scene; or so it would seem. The other women that I had looked upon so distastefully, would be present in this life also. I not only had to work things out with Johnny, I would have to deal with these other women, who in this lifetime, may look upon *me* with arch criticism.

The possibilities in this type of analysis were somewhat frightening. In the best case scenario, I chose to believe that I would always be the victor. I chose this scenario only because it seemed a logical explanation to my being given the opportunity of wedlock to the man I had waited for across the corridors of time. I was convinced that all would work out well.

Only time would tell.

My lessons in reincarnation did not stop at this point. Another dream was presented shortly thereafter.

DREAM... I am a young Native American Indian lad. I am playing down at the stream with some of the other young boys. Tepees abound within my view. I look up to see an older Indian Man heading down a path which will lead him right past us.

I greatly admire this man. He is a Wise One and well respected within our community.

Someone told me that this Wise One gets his wisdom from somewhere high in the mountains and I wonder where? I am enthralled by the tales he tells and the knowledge he possesses. I want to find out where he is getting this information; who he is talking to.

Every morning, early, the Wise One leaves the campground and swiftly heads up into the mountains. I decided that one day I would follow him so I can see what provides the Wise One with all he possesses.

The opportunity arose swiftly and I now find myself trying to stay out of view as I follow the Wise One on his daily journey. The morning is heavy with fog and I have a terrible time keeping up with him.

At one point on this uphill trek, we are walking among aspen or birch, trees with a great deal of white bark. I strongly suspect they were birch as I remember more black on the bark than would be on aspen.

It is autumn. There are a lot of yellow leaves on the ground. The air is chilly and the fog turns into a heavy mist as we proceed further up the mountain.

I know that we are reaching the top because I can see more patches of sky through the trees. The fog and mist are lifting. I have never been up here before, but am not afraid.

I feel that no one will know that I have followed the Wise One as I have no plans to speak of this.

The Wise One pauses near the edge of the woods and then steps up close to the rim of the mountain's cliff as I watch. He raises his arms skyward and tilts his head back slightly.

I wait anxiously to see who or what is going to appear.

To my surprise the Wise One cries in agony! I am astonished. I suddenly realize the Wise One has no one to talk to; no one in our camp that he can share his great knowledge with! So much wisdom is his, and his alone; I know this! I do not want what he has! I am so sad. I am sorry that I have followed him. I never knew he was so lonely.

Before I was even fully awake, I knew that the Wise One was, once again, my husband, Johnny. What does that young Indian boy have to work out with the older Indian?

I don't know.

I wasn't told.

But, I was left with the impression that it had to do with my deep felt desire to partake in the greatness of the Wise One's mind. I wanted what he had.

As a child, I expected I could have what the Wise One had; get it from the same place that he had; high in the mountains; that it would simply be there for the taking. I did not know that this extraordinary gift was not available to just anyone, and that it brought with it a cruel companion... mental isolation.

The Wise One's screams of agony pierced my heart and in an awakened state, renewed a memory long since forgotten: wisdom equals loneliness and I want no part of it.

At that time, it was not possible for the young Indian lad to have known how much loneliness was associated with a finely tuned, brilliant mind. He only desired knowledge and wisdom, having no idea that they came at a high price.

Across the ages, this Indian lad has held to the sight he came to witness on that mountain top, and shudders at the thought of being surrounded by throngs of people; yet, having no one to speak to.

Once again, as my mind reviewed the concept of reincarnation, I wondered if a nation could have karma, just like humans?

Was it possible for an entire race of people to have karma?

Do certain regions of the world have a karma regardless of whether there is a nation, kingdom, or small village residing in that area?

How about minerals such as gold and silver or maybe, even gem stones?

I believe they do, but the idea will need further study.

If this is true, what is the karma for America and her inhabitants, and why?

In EDGAR CAYCE'S SECRETS OF BEAUTY THROUGH HEALTH, the author states that the continuity of life and reincarnation into this Earth plane is an accepted fact by a majority of the world's population. The Native American Indian is taught this as a child; while in the East, it is part of the religious teachings also. Once a part of the early teachings of Christianity, all references to reincarnation were removed from the Holy Scriptures by the Byzantine emperor Justinian (483-565 A.D.), although more specifically, the entire belief system of the Christian Church was edited by and for Empress Theodora during the reign of her husband, Emperor Justinian.

If this is true, how sad that this information has been withheld from the public for some fifteen hundred years; thereby, promoting ignorance and suspicion all these years.

Again, if true, how many innocent human lives have been lost for their belief in reincarnation these past many years; died at the hands of their fellow beings for heresy based on the whim of one Empress named Theodora?

Chapter 9

JUDGE US NOT TOO HARSHLY

I volunteered to be a Den Mother once again, and a Girl Scout Leader, too. Of course, the elementary school needed another Room Mother; I simply couldn't pass up the chance to sing in the church choir; and other volunteer work crept in for various non-profit organizations. Life wouldn't be complete without having a child in the school band, on the football team, running cross-country, or track team, horseback riding or all of the above at once.

I loved our busy schedule.

But one day, after watching me race around, trying to get everyone to their appropriate activity on time, my husband asked if there was anything he could do to help.

Half jokingly, I replied, "Yeah, a chauffeur would be nice."

We both laughed at my flippant answer, knowing full well that within these words lay more truth than fiction.

However, amidst all this commotion, my courtier and dream companion did not forget me. He still made his visits.

One beautiful morning as I picked up the newspaper, I suddenly became ill and felt nauseous. I was confused because only moments before I had been perfectly well.

Quickly, I realized it was not actually *me* who was ill; it was my unseen companion. I knew that somewhere within this newspaper lay a serious problem. As I cautiously scanned the pages, from top to bottom, I knew he would direct me to the article that concerned him, and I would be permitted to discover the cause of his discomfort.

The date on The Atlanta Constitution read September 13, 1970; nothing seemed significant there. I skimmed past several articles paying no attention to any one particular topic. The Vietnam War drew a lot of attention these days due to considerable publicity surrounding a massacre that had taken place in the small hamlet of My Lai (pronounced "Me Lie"); but, personally, I felt no real involvement in this war since none of my family had been called into service. I never understood why we got involved anyway?

Traveling through more articles, I pondered the nation's opinion poles concerning this jungle war involvement and wondered if it was really true; what many people had to say?

Was this war little more then a political ploy; oust one player; bring in another? Were our men mere gun "fodder" for the politically astute who were not allowing us to fight seriously; not allowing us to win?

I did not know any of this to be a fact and wondered where I could find truth in the matter? These utterances, logged in the recesses of my mind, were merely a collection of public opinion poles and memories of expressed concerns during social gatherings.

Bringing my mind back into focus on the issue at hand, I found that having passed over much of the material on the war, I was experiencing an urgent need to go back.

But, back to what?

I had obviously overlooked something.

Seeking advice, I was alerted to the fact that the backward search was not too far away. It seemed only to encompass the previous page. Searching more carefully now, my eyes halted on an article referencing the arrest of a Lieutenant W.L. Calley.

Then the voice began to speak, his words filled with sadness and hurt. I had obviously found the intended article that brought about his illness. The Advocate spoke:

Today seems to mark the beginning of the end. Oh, America how I cry for thee! You, too, were like Israel when Israel was a child. But you too like Israel have forsaken Truth and Virtue and are holding hands with Death. Your Beauty has left you from your adulterous ways. Liars are your constant companions. No longer are you able to hold high your head amongst your foes, for yours is a Coward's lot. Where are those who loved you? Gone. All gone with Time. Where are those who fought with the Almighty at their side that your name could not be scandalously whispered among the shadows? Gone. Gone to a Hero's grave.

- The Advocate

It was evident that this nation had just hung itself. The Advocate ceremoniously stated, "**Today seems to mark the beginning of the end. Oh, America how I cry for thee!**" His anguish is obvious.

I have no idea what the truth was behind the scenes of this war, nor where matters of truth could be found with regards to this reported massacre. I only knew what the news media had presented and something was not right.

There had been a blood bath; an outrageous slaughter of old men, women, children and babies at this village and someone had to pay. This was not to say there were no other massacres, nor was it to say that Lt. Calley had not taken part in it; just that the news media had gotten a hold on this one and wasn't about to let it die. The news media had not been apprised of the complete story; the whole truth.

The morning paper stated that a Lt. Calley had directed this slaughter. An American soldier, a protector of his people, was being arrested as responsible for this ignoble deed. But it was indisputable, based on the adamant concerns of The Advocate, that this action was not entirely appropriate. As a matter of fact, something was critically wrong.

I have no idea what The Advocate meant in referencing "**Israel**" when he stated: "**You, too, were like Israel when Israel was a child. But you too, like Israel have forsaken Truth and Virtue and are holding hands with Death.**" I am not familiar with the political aspects of the Israeli people, particularly as seen through the eyes of The Advocate, but, do know that they too, have been warned in the past about their corruptible actions and impure thoughts.

I am also aware, that this young nation of America was seen by many of its founding fathers and early poets as being a "chosen" nation; thereby, making Americans a "chosen" people. They had high hopes for its purity and integrity as well as its devoted service to a mighty God.

Maybe we both started out with a strong spirit of righteousness, convinced that we were indestructible with the Almighty on our side. Maybe neither of us noticed when we began to wander from the truths we once held so dearly; but we certainly have wandered a far distance from our original inception.

The Advocate makes it quite clear in his statement, "**have forsaken Truth and Virtue and are holding hands with Death,**" that he is referencing the incident concerning this young man named Lt. Calley.

The Advocate tells me that someone (or several someones) were lying and a "deal" was made; a cover-up had occurred.

"Why should this cover-up be of interest to The Advocate?" I quietly questioned my own mind, knowing full well that these situations have occurred in the past and will continue to occur as long as deals *can* be made.

"What was so special about this one?"

I silently vowed to seek solutions to my unanswerable questions at a later date, and brought my mind back into focus on the matter before me.

The Advocate continues his oration: "**Your Beauty has left you from your adulterous ways**."

Mr. Webster describes the word "adultery" as, "voluntary sexual intercourse between a married man and someone other than his wife or between a married woman and someone other than her husband."

In contrast, The Advocate reminds us that this nation and her people, used to be considered united. The people and their government "of the people" acted in one accord; they were joined in a marriage. But, at some point in this harmonious union, one of the parties began stepping out on the other; began "climbing in bed" with other entities for personal enjoyment.

This adulterous partner failed to honor the marriage vows and cared not if the mate was harmed. Personal gain was the only motive.

Our leaders are to be considered the adulterous partners which have caused our beauty to fade; but we, the people, are following closely in their footsteps. The "union" is in shambles.

The Advocate is saying that we will do *anything* for power and money. We have prostituted ourselves to other nations and have, consequently, paid a high price for our power-hungry arrogance. We have become unsightly. We are no longer the raving beauty to which kings and queens the world over paid glorious tribute.

We are told that "**Liars are your constant companions**" and "**no longer can you hold high your head amongst your foes, for yours is a coward's lot...**"

We are being forced to face a couple of situations here, directly related to our young lieutenant. For one, someone (or several someones) have deliberately misled the American public into a particular thinking; they have lied to us. People we have trusted, people in places of authority, people whose word we have never doubted, have not told us the truth; these "**Liars**" make up the "**constant companions**" with which we keep company.

These same people will do whatever it takes to clear themselves of any wrong doing, no matter who they hurt along the way. And, in an effort to maintain their illustrious careers, will feed us words of comfort that have no truth to them.

Lt. Calley was verbally "hanged" by the very military service under which he served. The military then released selected tidbits of information to the public, through the news media, stating whatever information they wanted the public to hear, and suppressed the rest.

Secondly, when The Advocate asserts that "**no longer can you hold high your head amongst your foes, for yours is a coward's lot...**" we are informed that even our enemies know of our lying, deceitful manner and they plainly see us as cowards. But, this new accusation is frightening for it clearly indicates our foe is fully aware of our misconduct, not only in this affair, but others as well. They may have been co-conspirators.

Our "**foe**" is acutely aware of what really took place that day and whatever took place both before and after the incident. It indicates further, that our "**foe**" knew of our "internal" cover-up and viewed us with disdain. Lieutenant Calley was merely the sacrificial lamb.

But why, and for what purpose?

Somehow, somewhere, the leaders of this beautiful country had goofed and a public sacrifice was being made. The news media helped create this sacrificial lamb without knowing the full extent of the problem.

Being a soldier, however, who was Lt. Calley taking direction from, or was he left alone to make this monumental decision of destruction, and if so, why? Was this military son paying the price for the many indiscretions of his own country's leaders?

The Advocate says "yes."

"**Where are those who loved you? Gone. All gone with Time. Where are those who fought with the Almighty at their side that your name could not be scandalously whispered among the shadows? Gone. Gone to a Hero's grave.**"

MP Questions Driver of Car Which Drove Past Court

geans appeared to have more sympathy for Lt. William Calley's plight than his fellow officers.

In a random survey here on this sprawling infantry center, it was the West Pointer, the professional soldier and career man who was most outspoken in suggesting the jury's finding that Calley is guilty of premeditated murder at My Lai.

Many young officers of Calley's own rank agreed that he should be convicted and punished for his actions at My Lai, where he killed at least 22 unarmed Vietnamese, according to the jury's verdict.

The jury made the right decision, 10 out of 12 lieutenants said in one poll.

Some of those who gave opinions asked that their names not be used because, as one young lieutenant said, "I got to get along with my sergeants."

One second lieutenant disagreed with the verdict, philosophizing, "In a sense that I feel very strongly, Lt. Cal...

Didn't Kill Wantonly --Calley

By PHIL GAILEY
Constitution Staff Writer

FT. BENNING, Ga.—Addressing the six Army officers about to decide if he will live or die, Lt. William Calley, wracked with emotion and gasping for breath, said he has never "wantonly" killed "a human being in my entire life."

Standing in the middle of the red - carpeted courtroom facing the solemn jurors, Lt. Calley began, "Your honor, court members, I asked Mr. Latimer and my other attorneys not to go into mitigation in this case.

"There are a lot of things which are really not appropriate and I don't think it really matters what kind of individual I am. And I'm not going to stand here and plead for my life and my freedom, but I would ask you to consider a thousand lives that are going to be lost in Southeast Asia—a thousand more to be imprisoned, not only in present here in the United States, but in North Vietnam and hospitals all over the world as amputees.

"I've never known a soldier — nor did I ever myself — ever wantonly kill a human being in my entire life.

"If I have committed a crime, the only crime I have committed is in a judgment of my values. Apparently, I valued my troops' lives more than I did that of the enemy.

"When my troops were getting massacred and mauled by an enemy I couldn't see, I couldn't feel, I couldn't touch — that nobody in the military system ever described as anything other than communism. They didn't give it a race. They didn't give it a sex. They never let me believe

if was just a philosophy in a man's mind.

"That was my enemy out there. And when it became between me and that enemy, I had to value the lives of my troops and feel that is the only crime I have committed.

"Yesterday," he concluded, tears in his eyes and his voice cracking, "you stripped me of all my honor. Please — by your actions that you take here today — don't strip failure of soldiers of their honor—I beg of you."

With that, Lt. Calley, who was convicted Monday of the premeditated murder of at least 22 South Vietnamese civilians at My Lai three years

See CALLEY, Page 10-A

Senator Thurmond Sees Daughter

GREENWOOD, S.C. — Sen. Strom Thurmond, 68, is relieved in the nursery glass at Self Memorial Hospital Tuesday as he sees his first child, a girl, for the first time. His wife Nancy, 23, was reported in good condition. (Associated Press Wirephoto)

Lock
Acc

NEW YORK (NYT) — The British government and the Lockheed Aircraft Corp. conditionally agreed Tuesday on terms for keeping alive the Rolls-Royce jet engine developed for Lockheed's three air bus.

It was the first break in international aviation circles that came to the surface when Rolls went into receivership because of excess costs on the engine.

The terms, it Lockheed spokesman said, must now be submitted to the partners have ordered the 20-now get airliner and to the financing the sales. This be done starting Wednesday.

The tentative agreement was drawn up in board meetings in Washington. In turn revolved around British offer relayed from a cabinet meeting Monday.

The two-sentence Lockheed announcement gave no idea what the terms might be but would company official any details.

In the last week, s...

Some Draft Boards Quit Over Ca

**By GREGORY JAYNES
and GENE STEPHENS**

Several draft board members, agreeing they "don't have the stomach" to induct men as they can "come home to be hanged," resigned Tuesday while a south Georgia sheriff said he would not arrest AWOL soldiers in his county. Two other boards balked.

The five members of the draft board in Athens — all World War II veterans — resigned after sending a letter to Gen. Mike Y. Hendrix, state Selective Service director, saying:

"We find the conviction of Lt. (William) Cal-

ley to be unacceptable, and cannot in good conscience continue to make decisions that will affect the lives and well being of our young men."

In Blairsville, the three members of the draft board resigned because, as chairman Robert E. Colwell said, "I don't want any part and I'm not going to have any part in drafting boys and sending them over there in Vietnam and having them treated the way Calley's been treated. This is the worst thing that's ever happened in the United States."

Resigning with Colwell are Tom B. Burnett and Aaron Hood. All three are World War II veterans.

In Baker County, Sheriff L. W. Gibson called The Atlanta Constitution Tuesday to urge all servicemen "to run away from them but. I'll protect them any way this Calley thing is cleared up."

Johnson, who said he's sending Calley's defense, said, "everybody, and white, feel the man is being crucified. It's got to be done or we'll have here in our country."

Quitman board members were Nixon and members of Congress to induct no more men.

George H. Pugh, chairman of C...

VERDICT PROTESTS POUR IN

State Congressmen Swamped

By BOB HURT
Constitution Washington Bureau

WASHINGTON—Georgians reacted Tuesday to the Calley

by the fact that sentiment is thus far 100 per cent one-sided.

U.S. Sen. Herman E. Talmadge characterized the...

to submit to the draft but is freed on appeal bond.

Talmadge's office received about 50 telegrams by Tuesday afternoon. Landrum's af...

they considered, that Calley was being made a "scapegoat" and should not be punished unless higher-up military authorities are also tried.

I have spoken with many Armed Services personnel who served in World War II. They expressed great disappointed in the lack of pride that seems to currently exist for, and among our fighting forces. They believe that World War II was the last time the people of this nation fully stood behind its war efforts with head held high. They blame the leadership (or lack thereof) for deterioration among the ranks.

I don't believe our heroic defenders are all gone, but I understand what The Advocate is trying to say. Heroes stand with us everyday as they race to the aid of victims surrounded by fire, flood, thievery, local catastrophe, war, etc.

The point The Advocate is trying to make here, is that our leadership is sorely lacking. We need some heroes. We are not united. If we continue to remain divided, we will fall.

Some six months passed by. Thoughts of Easter preparation crowded my mind as I glanced at the calendar noting the date: March 31, 1971.

Once again, upon bringing the newspaper into the house, I found my mood drastically changing. This time I did not feel ill. Instead, I was overwhelmed with a sense of great sadness.

Based on the earlier newspaper incident regarding Lt. Calley, I knew The Advocate was not pleased with yet, another issue and would soon direct me to the cause of his concern.

He sent me on a brief search and directed my eyes to this same Lt. Calley. This lieutenant had been put on trial before a military court, and found guilty as charged. Once again, The Advocate spoke:

Oh, Nation of Sorrow; who caused you to weep? T'was thine own kin. Poor son! A victim of time you have become. Rise up you foolish men and strike back before your foe holds you securely in his hands. Your God has withdrawn and hides His face from view. Yours is the fate of Rome... a boasting, wasteful, Godless Rome.

- The Advocate

We are addressed as a "**Nation of Sorrow.**" We are expected to be in mourning.

85

We are asked by The Advocate "**who caused you to weep?**" and are answered by the all-knowing voice, "**T'was thine own kin.**"

With these words, we can be sure the true offender lies within the boundaries of our own country, among our own military leaders; where I later learned that even President Nixon was appalled by the action taken against this simple soldier and wanted to put a stop to the trail. Strong advice from his counselors caused him to remain aloof.

Lieutenant Calley was, as stated before, a scapegoat for higher officials, and is addressed as "**Poor son!**" The Advocate also states this soldier was "**a victim of time**" and place in the context of this war. Something took place either at the time he entered military service, while he was in training, after he became an officer, or all of the above.

Not being satisfied with my own lack of knowledge surrounding these matters referenced by The Advocate, I chose to look into the subject massacre for the purpose of this book and found good reading in THE COURT-MARTIAL OF LT. CALLEY written by Richard Hammer.

Mr. Hammer gives us excellent background information, methodically pointing to the destined path of this young man through a series of misguided steps, both contrived of his own choosing and by the actions of others. Twenty-five men were originally charged with involvement in the incident at My Lai, including two generals. One by one the men were released, all but "Rusty" Calley.

Of course, the generals' careers were essentially over due to the scandal, both men being stripped of their Distinguished Service Medals. But, that was pretty much it. General Young retired with full pension in June, 1971.

Of all those charged, Lt. Calley was the only one left to face the barrage of accusations dealing with orders to "search and destroy" one village suspected to house the enemy. Even though it was known the night before the attack that this area, once thought to house Viet Cong, only housed "friendly" forces, the attack proceeded as planned. An exaggerated after-action report filed by the Task Force commander indicated a stupendous victory over a major enemy, when, in fact, they were old men, women, children and babies.

One hundred twenty-eight (128) villagers were killed that day with only three (3) guns being captured. If this truly was a "stupendous victory", what happened to all the firearms the villagers should have had?

So, wherein lies the fault?

It is not quite that easy to answer.

The answer is multi-faceted and requires another book just to explain the complicated reporting operation of the military, and I have not been charged with that task. I have just been asked to bring your attention to the gross errors in which our system operates, in the high hopes that we, the people, will take a stand for righteousness; not to take so much at face value. Look deeper; search for truth; defend honesty.

The Advocate cautions us to awaken and be ready to defend ourselves before "**your foe holds you securely in his hands.**"

This "**foe**" may be found among our nation's own leaders; he may be crouching just outside the doors of this country on foreign soil, or he may be found within the darkest recesses of the human mind. We must remember that our foe can come in many disguises and catch us unaware. We, therefore, must remain ever watchful.

Again, I think Richard Hammer states it well when he says, "We have come a long way from those innocent and moralistic days of World War II, when we knew we were in the right and that the enemy was evil and had to be destroyed. In Vietnam, at My Lai, America lost its innocence. We had thought that somehow, some way we were better than other people. When we fought wars, it was never for national aggrandizement, never for gain, but for the weak and the oppressed, to free them from their bonds of tyranny. If war crimes were committed, if atrocities were perpetrated, it was always the other side that did them, not Americans......We forgot, or ignored, the clearing of the Indians from the western plains...... Americans believed fully that Americans were the good guys and the other side the bad guys. Maybe we were better in those days with our naivete, our sense of mission, the sense that we were devoted to principle. We were innocents at large in the world, stumbling and bumbling but thinking that we were trying to do good.

Vietnam and My Lai have ended American's innocence, ended it perhaps for good."

Commenting on the book by Richard Hammer, the New York Post states "...Weep for what the war in Viet-Nam has done to the Vietnamese, to the Americans sent in to 'save' them, and our good name in the world."

The Advocate jumps in to say that we are no longer the America that once had the Almighty fighting by its side. When we stand on the battle field, we stand alone. We are told, **"Your God has withdrawn and hides His face from view."**

There was a time when we were referred to as arrogant and wasteful. For a long time we were even called the "ugly" American. But we have enjoyed our riches and really didn't care what others said or thought about us.

The Advocate states we are on the downhill side of prosperity, wisdom, virtue and faithfulness. We are falling, just like Rome; **"a boasting, wasteful, Godless Rome."**

What price will we have to pay to a Higher Power for our arrogance and disobedience?

Later that same day, as evening settled in, I went to my desk and wrote a tearful prayer admitting to the Great One that I was frightened. This world was not mine; I did not understand it; I wanted to come home. The road had become long and hard and I was growing weary. I asked for my tears to be dried and my broken heart to be mended, then slowly put my pencil down.

Saddened by my prayer, The Advocate responded immediately, and cried loudly on behalf of America and its people as he addressed **"Nations of Foreign Soil."**

He became the spokesperson for these United States as he pleaded with an all-knowing mind to the other nations he knew all too well.

Judge us not too harshly, Oh Nations of Foreign Soil, but grieve with loud weeping for ours is none other than the ill fate you all suffered so long ago. Hear our moans, and have great pity. Review your own histories before you point accusingly at us for we are but remnants of your past. We are the offspring of your mistakes, only we seem to have multiplied in Disease of Mind, Cruelty of Tongue, and in Abomination of Law. When you hear our bones cry out, pray loudly that the angels may know of our suffering; for we have walked the very streets of Hell.

- The Advocate

This oration was not in response to any question that I had asked. This was simply expressed as a complimentary grieving to the prayer I had just offered. The Advocate cried out to the other nations of the world not to judge this young, willful nation with too much severity. The other nations are asked to grieve and rend their clothing for us as the fate we are about to encounter is none other than the ill fate that they all suffered long ago.

The mediating voice begs the other nations to hear the pain in our tortured cries; the cries of a nation near death. And when this pain is understood The Advocate asks that foreign lands have great pity on us.

The Advocate tells the nations on distant soils to review their own histories before they begin pointing fingers at us because we were once a part of them. Everything we have said and done reflects back to the lands that produced our forefathers' fathers.

But, The Advocate goes further to say, we have only made matters worse. Once thought to be the brave, new Promised Land, we have failed miserably and become equivalent to the "black sheep" of the family. We are the vulgar relatives who are not invited to dine for fear of embarrassing the guests. We are an embarrassment to the ancestors who bore us.

The Advocate makes a plea for America and her inhabitants. He speaks of the pain and suffering we have caused ourselves, and begs that these nations across the oceans and adjacent to our fertile soils, hear our cries and pray for us. He asks these nations to pray for us based on their own past mistakes and to understand the misguided steps of a young nation. He asks that they pray loud enough in the grand hopes that their prayers reach the heavens where the angels may hear.

This nation, called America, has invited Hell to her doorstep and descended to great depths to meet evil on its own terms. The Advocate states, **"We have walked the very streets of Hell."** Other nations have done likewise; he only asks that they remember this and have great pity on us.

Chapter 10

A SEASON OF CHANGE

My unseen companions have never faltered in their strategic communication program with this earthly recipient... me. As time passed, however, their transmittals created an uneasiness for me, due to my own strong sense of guilt.

I had failed to move forward with my assigned project. I had made no real effort to place their messages before the people they so dearly loved. I, and I alone, was to blame.

I have to admit, I simply did not know what to do. Yes, I knew I was to write a book, and yes, I had a title for the collective works; but, what steps are necessary in writing a book?

What formalities are required?

What about copyrights?

If I reference some else's work and quote them, do I really have to get their permission in writing?

How do you get the attention of a publisher? Can I just send them a copy of my completed manuscript?

I knew, at some point, I would have to seriously search for appropriate help, but, it never occurred to me to ask this beautiful Force for such advice. I offered no prayers in this matter. Instead, I choose to venture forth, showing a bit of bravery now and then, sharing some of my prophetic dreams with carefully chosen friends and relatives and speaking of my frustration in finding a publisher. I hoped someone would help me out.

There were certain matters revealed to me that I knew others would find difficult to comprehend, so I kept those tidbits of information to myself for the time being. It was best not to speak on these topics until the atmosphere was properly prepared for better reception. Too much hurt had already been encountered through tongue lashings, scripture quoted in little messages mailed to my house, and certain so-called "friends" no longer inviting me over for coffee and tea.

By venturing forth in this manner, I was actually testing the climate to see how well some of this material would be received by the public. In addition, I was acting like a solicitor, hoping to accumulate productive ideas as to publishing, or find someone who was acquainted with the industry and could provide assistance.

I had to admit, it certainly was frustrating to be in possession of so much remarkable information and not be able to proclaim it to vast audiences throughout the land. Perhaps, that is what the Indian, the Wise One, felt in a distant past when his heart and mind were overflowing with knowledge that no one else could understand.

But I held my tongue, allowing only brief bursts of discrete disclosure; living in fear of ridicule from those within my church and community. I even failed to speak of these matters with most of my relatives, dreading their disbelief in what I had to say.

One day, I finally decided to approach my Sunday School teacher and ask her advice on how to present the messages I was receiving. She taught the young adults and couples class and I perceived her as an open-minded individual. I had great confidence in her ability to reason. I firmly believed that she always spoke truth and was willing to look beyond current church doctrines, if the need presented itself.

That particular Sunday, I waited until nearly everyone had left our classroom. When she had spoken with the last person, I asked for a moment of her time. She responded, saying that her husband was waiting for her, and would it be possible for us to meet another time?

I was gravely disappointed. It had taken so much courage to simply make the decision to speak to her about my mysterious friends.

Seeing the disappointment in my face and sensing my frustration, she smiled and said that she knew her husband would wait. What did I have on my mind?

I was *so* relieved to be able to speak to someone other than family and close friends. She listened attentively as I told her of rejection upon rejection by both friends and relatives in regards to what I had to say. I told her that somehow I had to get these messages out and speak to the people, but based on the initial reactions from both family and friends, I did not think very many would listen. I asked her what I should do?

Her reply was simple and beautiful.

She first began her answer with a Bible quote, "**Don't cast your pearls among the swine, lest they trample them under foot and turn to attack you.**"

Then continued to say, "Dear, do not let people destroy the beauty that is yours. Do not let them discourage you. Save your pearls of wisdom for a time when men will understand what it is that you have to say. You will know when the time is right. You may have to wait a long time, but never lose confidence in yourself and the mission that has been set before you."

I did not attend the church service that day; I was too excited. I wandered around the immense halls of the Peachtree Presbyterian Church; this church that boasted a congregation of well over 2000, living in pure joy.

This was my church home. I was comfortable here. My Sunday School teacher had just given me the much needed boost of confidence that was important to spur me on. I would collect the children after the church service and head for home. This would be a glorious day!

And so it was.

Day after day passed as my mind floated on its own clouds of happiness, greeting each new day with greater enthusiasm. The sun seemed brighter, the flowers smelled ever so sweet and the rippling waters flowing in the creek behind our house seemed to renew my spirit as never before.

My Sunday School teacher had given me this light-hearted feeling, if only for a little while.

I found myself riding on a perpetual high, when suddenly the winds that bore me ceased to blow.

Crashing to Earth, as my peaceful flight was gravely interrupted, I was overwhelmed by a new proposition: we had to move.

Now, under normal circumstances, this would not have been viewed as a traumatic ordeal, but at this moment in my life it took my breath away.

It was not the children for which I felt concern; nor was it my husband. It was me.

I had just gained a serious ally in the form of my Sunday School teacher; a person who, I considered, a critical defender of my sanity. Here was a well-respected individual who seemed fully to understand my agony and ecstasy as the receiver of wondrous tidings from a world

93

unknown to most. Here was a women who had given me hope in a world where I was being slowly crushed.

What would I do without her?

Find another?

I didn't think that was possible. It took so long to find just this one gentle soul. I was seriously disappointed and wallowing in self-pity.

Atlanta had played hostess to us for four lovely years, but business opportunities move families around the country, like gypsies, and ours was no different.

Johnny and I were given a variety of states to choose from and we decided on Colorful Colorado. We reasoned that Denver would be the midway point for traveling relatives and friends between the east and west coasts, and thus, we should have lots of folks coming to visit.

Saying farewell to "the New York of the South," we headed west with a well planned itinerary. I drove one station wagon and Johnny drove the other with our jeep in tow.

It would not be reasonable to state that confusion reigned supreme upon our arrival in Colorado, but the accuracy of that statement is close.

Our new found environment was totally different than what our minds and bodies had so recently been accustomed; major adjustments were necessary.

Discussions with the moving company's dispatcher brought distressing news concerning the loss of one of our moving vans. It seems that it mysteriously vanished.

It was nowhere to be found.

For three full days this van was missing and finally turned up somewhere in Louisiana.

Why was it in Louisiana instead of Colorado?

Believe me, even after listening to the explanation given by the dispatcher I still didn't know. It made little sense to me.

The month was now August, 1972 and the air was hot and dry and a constant breeze blew that dried our skin and nostrils. I could plainly see that a moist atmosphere was not a known companion to these high plains.

Mountain peaks spiraled gloriously to meet the heavens in some type of seeming praise, while the green grasses that existed lacked the velvet consistency that our feet and toes had so much enjoyed in days now gone. The skies mirrored the blues of the aquamarine stones that my mother collected from the mines of Brazil; so unlike the shrouded atmosphere of the home we had just left.

We played the role of modest tourist for a few days, but preferred the coolness of our motel room to the outside environment, following the Summer Olympics with great enthusiasm. By the week's end, serious thought had to be given to registering all four children in their respective schools. Second on the agenda was getting warmer clothing for Colorado's anticipated arctic winters.

Once the registrations were complete, we took our time in the selection of clothing and decided to wait a while for the heavier garments. This determination was made since the season for winter was not within the near future; or so we thought.

Halloween arrived and so did our first Colorado snow storm. The kleenex-sized pieces of snow began to fall late that afternoon, and costumed children gazed through steamy windows with sheer disappointment written on their faces as night settled in.

To the delight of the little ones, their dad decided to drive them around for Trick 'r Treating in the family jeep to keep them from freezing. Moist, cold winds howled as delicate snowflakes were tossed fiercely for five full days.

Before our departure from Atlanta, I had agreed to be Johnny's secretary until he could hire another. The position would be at our house, so I would still be there for the children when they came home from school. I was not sure how I was going to like this additional job, but it would only be temporary; that's what I was told.

Slowly, I found myself missing the warmth of my caring, southern neighbor ladies. This new community was not what I would have called "friendly." I missed the occasional cups of freshly brewed coffee that I shared with my lady-friends during our mid-morning breaks from household chores.

In addition, I had much difficulty in finding little friends with whom our youngest child could play. I literally drove up, down and around both paved and dirt driveways; from house to house in search of playmates... *one* was available.

The children of this neighborhood had little free time. They were well programmed with lessons in tennis, skiing, piano or some other instrument. Ballet, gymnastics and scouts were crowded in too. So few of their mothers were even home. So many housekeepers and nannies dominated the homes of this neighborhood, I was not sure whether I was going to enjoy this place or not.

Time would have to provide me with an answer.

Time did pass with greater speed than anticipated. I stayed busy in my new job as secretary handling phone calls, salesmen's briefings, freight and UPS deliveries and filling small orders. This routine allowed me sufficient time to run my household with a little additional help. The new job did not drastically interfere with the children's activities or my need to be where they were at a given time.

Communication with my unseen friends was sporadic, although I fully recognized that it was I who was not adequately "tuned in." I still required more time to organize my household, adjust to this new job and feel comfortable with my new location on the prairie.

One night, feeling quite satisfied as to how the day had gone, I climbed into bed and ever so slowly, fell backwards onto the comfort of my king-sized mattress. Anticipation of sleep was foremost in my mind. I don't even remember my head touching the pillow when, without warning, I found myself standing at my bedside, looking down at my body lying on the bed.

DREAM/VISION/OUT-OF-BODY EXPERIENCE... **I am confused! I find myself standing beside my own bed, yet my feet are not touching the floor. I am standing free and weightless, no more than a yard above the carpeting.**

I look at my body as it lies resting on the bed where I have just been. I watch as my spirit slowly sits up and moves to unite with me beside the bed, leaving behind the collection of bones and body mass that I have known as "Nancy."

We are now joined together in complete oneness, my spirit and I. The body I have known as "Nancy" still rests undisturbed on the bed below and in front of me.

An awesome love and compassion for all things consumes me. I look at the body on the bed and hear myself say, "It has been a good body."

In some strange way I seem to be thanking this assemblage of flesh and bone for taking care of me; for providing me with housing. I don't know why.

The sounds of silence surrounding me are strangely musical. I know I belong to "It," and that "It" is somewhere behind me. "It" is my true "home."

I am totally free of anger, animosity, jealousy, all negative human emotion. I wait, in full expectation, to be whisked backwards; to become a part of that to which I know I belong. The procedure begins.

Suddenly, I find myself lying on my back, fully awake, in my own bed. After a quick surveillance of my surroundings, I find myself gravely disappointed to be back in body form.

I hear myself acknowledge this disappointment by exclaiming, "Rats!"

I have never felt such peace and harmony. Was it time for me to say "thank you" to my body for housing and caring for my soul?

Is this what we are all expected to do?

I don't know.

If this was truly an "out-of-body" experience for the purpose of demonstrating the entrance into another "corridor" of time, then I am pleased to have been chosen as the student of illustration.

If it was that Death and I exchanged an awareness of one another that night, it was truly strange. I have often wondered how it would feel to die; this feeling being strong in me now that so many around me have grown old and are leaving this Earth plane.

I have no fears now, for death is but a word, and a small one at that. I simply "crossed over" with no awareness of entry or exit.

It was a beautiful, peaceful experience.

The step from here to beyond is exactly that, a step.

If God's intention was to show me how simple this step through another "corridor," another "passage of time" can be, using this body as an example, then I no longer agonize over any soul who takes that step. It is so quick and peaceful.

Nothing exists on this Earth like that kind of peace.

Even as I write today, I still wonder how I would have appeared medically at that given moment when I stood beside myself, clearly divided into two separate beings.

Could it be that I was allowed to merely glance back into another one of my past lifetimes to once again "review" death that I might tell others?

I have no idea.

If it would have been my fate to have died that night, I would beg that no one cry. The world I drifted into was not of loneliness, pain and suffering. It held only the promise of a Holy Love that crossed all barriers of time.

Chapter 11

A NATION IN ANGUISH

Foolish man. Are you deaf as well as blind? Can you not hear the ancient prophets groan and cry? Can you not mark even the signs given by Mother Nature? Remember well... Israel has been reborn.

- The Advocate

The Advocate speaks forcefully of his apparent aggravation with mankind. He states that we are **"foolish,"** although he is actually more worried about us than irritated. From his viewpoint, we do little more than play. We ignore events that have been foretold for eons and continue to do just as we choose. We make no preparations spiritually and seem to have little concern for what we will do when the great disturbances occur within Mother Nature and the Earth, herself.

The Advocate cannot understand why we even *doubt* that the events will occur. Man's reasoning is beyond the comprehension of this unseen force. He cannot fathom why, even when man is warned, he does not take action; why he will not listen?

We, too, must understand the personage of this one called The Advocate. This voice is a force that acts in strict obedience to a power greater than itself. The Advocate is well versed in the functions and actions of man and is doing everything allowable to help save the creation known as humanity.

When The Advocate asks **"Are you deaf as well as blind?"** he wonders if we have lost the ability to both hear and see. Obviously, we can hear and see but fail to focus where this force wishes us to place our attention. His concern lies in two realms: (1) that we have repeatedly ignored the warnings given to us by the prophets of old and by our holy books, and (2) that we do not seem to heed the messages of change whispered to us by the winds and tides of Mother Nature, and concurrently, refuse to see the changes that are so evident.

He also states "**Can you not hear the ancient prophets groan and cry?**" Here he refers to the fact that long ago prophets foretold many of the events which are occurring, and are about to occur. They, too, warned man to get his act together because one day he would have to appear before the Highest Court known and account for his many actions or lack thereof.

This High Court to which we will be summoned does not exist on Earth, but on a much higher plane. It is within the free will of man to choose whether he will be prepared to appear in this Great Hall of Justice or not.

If we are to believe in reincarnation, could it be that many of these ancient prophets are here today, to once again warn us of these coming events?

The Advocate also says that the ancient prophets are in mourning for us; for mankind. They are rending (tearing) their "clothing" and crying for all of those who will not make it home because they refuse to listen.

When The Advocate states, "**Remember well--Israel has been reborn**" he is alerting us to the past warnings concerning this predicted event. We were told that mankind's accountability to a higher force, our own Creator, would take place when the Jews had been gathered into one place and had become a nation once again.

That event occurred in 1948 when Israel was founded, and a call went out to all parts of the world for Jews to come home; home to their long awaited Promised Land.

After the occurrence of this major historical event, we were told to watch for specific actions culminating in the rebuilding of the Temple in Jerusalem. The generation slotted for these world shattering events is us.

We are subtly told to "get our act together." We know that the ancient prophets not only warned us of coming catastrophic Earth changes, but also warned of the poor spiritual and moral habits of man and its dreadful consequences.

I think this nation is still in the party mood that existed at the time we were told to save our "**cereal**"; our grain. We act as if the festivities can go on forever without any consequences.

We know Israel has been reborn, but we take no action to secure our position.

I do not understand what it is within man that causes him to be such a procrastinator. We all seem to wait until the eleventh hour to accomplish that which we must.

But this time, our eleventh hour timing may be badly off.

The clock is approaching 11:59 o'clock in reference to the health of this nation and ourselves; twelve o'clock is our deadline.

The Advocate has no clock to watch and is quite capable of "bending" the time to suit the wishes of the Creator, if we are found worthy of such action.

As seen through the eyes of The Advocate, these forthcoming predicted events are not "set in concrete"; that is, we, the human race, are provided with the opportunity to change and modify the scheduled occurrences. We can "script" or re-write the coming events, just like a movie or play. We can actually cancel a world catastrophe by changing certain "acts" within the play.

The Advocate says, regarding this matter:

If it were not true, I would have told you.

- The Advocate

William Shakespeare was quite right when he told us, "All the World is a stage and we are but actors in it." We, mankind, assist in writing the script by which we are destined to live; Earth is our stage. Our Creator gives us the free will by which to "script" our own existence. We create our own misery and our own joy by our individual and collective thinking and actions. With enough collective goodwill thinking, and unselfish goodwill actions on the part of the majority, we can make a significant difference.

Don't let anyone tell you otherwise.

In his statement, "**If it were not true, I would have told you**" The Advocate again, has difficulty in understanding why we do not surge ahead and make the required changes knowing, full well, that we can and that our time is limited.

As stated before, he is not bound by the time constraints surrounding our Earth plane; we are. And because we are, we must act upon our new formed decisions with great haste. It requires only a

101

serious effort on our part to make these necessary changes; to modify our destiny.

The Advocate asks that we try a little harder to do what we know we must. He can help us, but we are required to make the first move; to use our own powers of free will. We must be motivated to change the circumstances that surround us in order to acquire a more desirable outcome. It cannot be forced upon us.

The Advocate has never used the word "lazy" in reference to our actions, or lack thereof, for the word, itself, denotes feebleness, weakness, sluggishness or none energetic. He has never seen this America as any of these.

He views us as willfully disobedient, knowing full well the consequences of our actions, and just not caring enough about the outcome. He hopes that his love for us can change our arrogant nature and insolence, and save us from a prescribed disaster. He views our in-action as a serious flaw within the nature of man, which he is trying to help us overcome.

One afternoon, a vastly irritated Advocate dynamically threw words at us in the hopes of initiating a reaction of total shock. His advice, his warnings and the warnings of so many others have gone on unheeded for generation after generation.

The Creator, Himself, has sent legions of angels, prophets and other spiritual Beings for eons in the hopes that guidance from these chosen entities would have a positive impact on the behavior of the human creation; but, little has changed.

We have failed to grow spiritually and are rapidly losing the battle for survival. This is what The Advocate has to say:

Hear me, O Nation of Sorrow! Thy thoughts have become rancid; the very marrow of thy bones as dust. Harken to the word of thy Father through the One Who Came Before us. Oh, where has thy bigotry led us? Who now will hold our hand? The earth rumbles in rage, and darkness seems so near. Oh foolish, cowardly man, with the backbone of a worm, how can thy Father even want thee?

- The Advocate

Now we have been directed to listen very closely to what he has to say by his command, **"Hear me!"** It has become graphically apparent that our thoughts and actions have not gone unnoticed, and we have displeased a higher authority. Someone is obviously more concerned about our well-being than we are.

The misery this Nation has been experiencing is what we have brought upon ourselves. No other is responsible. If we do not think we are in misery, then we truly have been deceived.

The Advocate then goes on with his carefully selected areas of concern; the reasons he feels we should be addressed as **"O Nation of Sorrow."**

First he states, **"Thy thoughts have become rancid."** The word "rancid" is seldom used anymore. In times past, when refrigeration was less available or non-existent, it described spoiled butter, lard (shortening) and oils. It was also used in reference to meat. No matter what the food product was that was declared "rancid," this particular word clearly stated the condition of the item and that it was unfit for consumption.

In our case, The Advocate has clearly spelled out the idea that man's thoughts have become EXTREMELY offensive; we are impossible to digest. Again, very specifically he is referencing *our* America. We are told that the thoughts of this nation, collectively, have become so offensive that they have been deemed worthless, they need to be thrown away. The Almighty One is about to turn away and listen no more!

The Advocate has not suggested that we get rid of America and its People altogether. He is simply stating that our current and past thought processes are no longer acceptable. It is imperative that we change our ways, lest we be destroyed. If we do not quickly choose to change our pattern of thinking, which has been resulting in some pretty poor actions, we can no longer expect help from the Great Beyond that has always been America's to claim.

Secondly he has stated, **"the very marrow of thy bones as dust."** He uses this term as illustration that the inner portion of our structural soundness is falling apart. This bone marrow keeps the "bone" structure alive. These "bones" of our body literally *hold us together*. We could not function without them; we would be doomed to a vegetative existence.

Therefore, when The Advocate makes reference to the marrow of our bones, he is speaking of the best, or choicest part, or essential portion, or even "innermost segment" of the very existence of this nation.

That is us; we, the people.

He is stating that the innermost segment, the very structure that gives us form, *has no more value then common, useless dust.* The word "dust" is known by all and needs no further clarification.

The Advocate is telling us that because our inner-most being (marrow) has reached a state of disintegration (dust), the United States, this America, has rendered itself useless; something to be cast off or thrown away; to be overthrown by an enemy.

The Advocate is trying to show us that these United States have no value in this beautifully created, cohesive and harmonic universe, given our current pattern of thinking and action. We are merely remnants of what, at one time, may have had value. We are a disgrace to what we were intended to be, and a disgrace to the kingdom from which we came.

It would serve us well to remember that we, the people, who form these United States, are the marrow of her bones. It is we, the people, who must take a stand to save ourselves and our land.

This America, these lands, have served us well and it is we who have put her in jeopardy. We have supported many wrong doings by the simple act of turning our heads away and pretending that we do not see. We are no longer permitted to act in this manner.

The rancid thoughts must first be discarded. Then we must take our "innermost segment," the essential portion, the choicest part, which is us, the people, and become a cohesive group in order to hold our America together.

The voice of The Advocate calls out in a loud manner and demands, **"Harken to the word of thy Father through the One Who Came Before us."**

At this point, The Advocate is almost calling on the trumpets of the Great Beyond to bring forth a majestic proclamation in order to bring the inhabitants of America to attention.

For the Christian, he speaks of Jesus of Nazareth, whom we call the Christ, when he references **"the One Who Came Before us."** He suggests that we listen attentively to the words of wisdom that were presented to us by that Being.

This Son of the Most High was sent as an example of what mankind was intended to be and clarified laws by which man was intended to live.

He also warned us of impending disaster, given the inherent nature of man. But, He gave us fair notice, so that we might have a chance to make necessary changes before final judgement for our childish actions is declared.

"**Oh, where has thy bigotry led us?**" he angrily asks. Here, The Advocate is unmistakenly pointing to our hypocritical nature; our obstinacy, our devotion to one thought; our single-mindedness.

With grave certainty, one can quickly point to the atrocities committed within the grounds of this young nation when we look at the manner in which we have treated our own native peoples.

We could look into our distant past to show how we have interfered in the affairs of foreign governments with the ultimate hope that they would be under one control; OURS! But that is not necessary. We need only look to the last few years.

We have not stepped in to see justice prevail. We have stepped in for profit, whether it be for monetary gain or political power. Most often, it has been the latter.

We're being offered Top Value Stamps again!

In some cases, we actually denied support to other countries such as Rhodesia (an English holding), sighting their views on slavery as the cause. The Russians discretely supported the opposing forces and Rhodesia fell with a bang.

Why did we not assist England with her holding? Could we simply not find enough political gain for ourselves? Was slavery the real issue? Speaking with a few of those Africans who fought for Rhodesia and lost, and witnessing the results of this loss by visiting the newly formed Zimbabwe some years ago, I again question our motives. Knowing the way we operate, we must have found it more politically astute to allow the English ruling authorities to fail; empowering the new entities with a takeover.

The Advocate has pointed to our lack of willingness to view another's concept; to accept another's separateness. And he asks "**Where has it led us?**"

I am instructed that acting exclusively; without collective thought; and lacking harmony with all brothers who believe in the One Great Spirit, we have caused much bickering and bloodshed for ourselves and others.

It is not our differences that we should be focusing on, but rather on what we have in common. We should have enough thoughtfulness to seek the beauty in another individual or nation. We should join forces so that we can be a part of the symphony that plays throughout the universe.

My son, Chris asked me, "How do we choose between two evil sides?" And I had to sadly reply, "I don't know."

My unseen companions had not prepared me for such a question and I felt completely helpless in providing him with a suitable answer.

The Advocate goes on to ask, "**Who will hold our hand**?"

In the use of the word "**us**," as in "**Where has it led us**?" and the word "**our**," he is trying to show us that even though he is angry and frustrated with this nation and her people, he is still willing to make a stand with and for us.

We are told, now that our thoughts are foul and our bones cannot hold us up, we are in decay; obviously rotten and living in a vegetative state. Further more, we stink!

On top of that, we are bigots!

So, the Advocate is asking who wants us?

I believe there are foreign nations who don't mind our stench. They "play" with us all the time. They like what we have to offer. And, because we have accumulated so many "playmates" we would be wise to use extreme caution as to who we identify as a true friend.

Fortunately for us, I again believe that we really do have some honest friends among these foreign nations who are kind enough to overlook our smell and poor manners. They have been hoping that we would eventually clean ourselves up so they could get a better look at us. We have been dirty all too long. These friends may well have forgotten the beauty that lies beneath all the filth. Maybe we could surprise them by becoming strong and beautiful once more.

In the next statement, the Advocate is getting down to much broader terms and actually references two things here. First, the Advocate states a *fact* when he says that the "**The earth rumbles in rage and darkness seems so near**."

A cleansing process, of sorts, has begun. During this process, old volcanos will re-ignite and new ones will form. In the worse case scenario, their explosions will cause the skies to darken for years. But we can change this, to a lesser time-frame, if we can correct our misconduct before we reach a point-of-no-return.

My unseen friends have told me that it is time for the Earth to make some rather significant changes herself. She does this periodically as a kind of growth and cleansing process; a growth for herself in her own evolution, and a cleansing process to rid herself of pollutants. Man is currently a pollutant; has been in the past, and will have to be thrown off if he does not change.

We are like fleas on a dog; a real irritant.

In more specific terms, I have been told that man's ugly thoughts (man's rancid thoughts) have actually caused fractures (rips) in the Earth, just as in a piece of cloth. In addition to this, we cause ruptures in the atmosphere above the Earth, which in turn, create weather disruptions. These atmospheric disturbances affect the Earth, AND also have a rippling effect far out into our own galaxy.

I do not pretend to understand exactly how this happens, but the rips are actually like wounds.

They are very real!

Let us look at this in another way... referred to as the Gaia Principle (or Gaia Hypothesis).

"Gaia" is the name given to the spirit of the Earth by the early Greeks. It was believed by many ancient cultures that the Earth was a living deity. She possessed a body which all men could see and housed an intelligence which men could not see.

We are to view the Earth as a living, breathing entity with her own identity. She has life and she has a soul. Everything created, minerals included, draw their strength from this lovely spirit. We are told that this Earth spirit receives her nourishment from the stars, and in turn, gives nourishment to all the living things she protects in her womb. When she reaches "the fullness of her time" (is about to give birth) through the spirit high above, she then gives birth to the minerals in her womb; not unlike a human mother bringing forth her newborn child.

Another way to look at this, also, is to consider that she (the Earth) is about to give birth (so we are told); birth to a whole new world. This birth causes much pain (for herself and everyone else), and the gases and fluids rumbling within her bowels (under the Earth's crust) can be heard if we will just take the time to listen.

People in Taos, New Mexico; Denver, Colorado and North Central Nebraska have been listening.

Referencing the word "**darkness**" once again, we find that it can be directly associated with the influence of the evil forces on man and fundamental behavior of mankind as a whole. The Advocate is stating that the "shade is being drawn" on the human population and man is about to be "snuffed out" if he is not more careful.

Being forewarned MANY Times previously by those sent to guide us, The Advocate now not only calls us "**foolish**," but "**cowardly**." Webster's dictionary says that the word "cowardly" means ignoble, lacks courage or yields to fear.

I don't think we yield to the fear of wrath from our Creator, or we would have mended our ways long ago. I think our cowardliness lies in our inability to do what we know is right. We are easily persuaded by those of ignoble intentions, and follow a path to further corruption.

We, the People of these United States, who are the bone marrow of America, have allowed corruption for a long, long time. The smell of money holds us captive. We have nearly sold our souls. We *have* prostituted our homeland.

My unseen friend goes on to say that we have "**the backbone of a worm**." This explanation is quite simple: the worm has no backbone!

"**How can thy Father even want thee?**" the voice demands in an attempt to shock us into change. But, we are told over and over again: He still does.

In summation, we are shown to be in pretty bad shape. But, as awful as we are (this does not mean "full of awe" as the word was first intended) we are still loved.

We, the people, who make up this America, are still loved by the Creative Force.

It is calling to us.

We must answer.

Chapter 12

ENTER THE FATHER

I had not yet met **THE FATHER**. The Advocate and his companions were the only ones who had been playing the role of teacher and protector during my many travels and adventures on both this Earth plane and other places quite foreign to me.

Before this Great Being made Himself known, I was taken on a journey into the past to review circumstances found nowhere in recorded history; at least not to which we are formally introduced. It was after this excursion that this Great One announced His arrival.

DREAM... **I have no idea exactly where on the North American continent we were when the dream started, but found myself positioned firmly on the ground, looking forward, beyond the vast horizon in a direction approximately North by Northwest.**

Soon, a rather large, round, white object became visible to the right of the distant horizon and sailed past this terrestrial ball to the left. I have no idea whether this particular object was our moon or another object from far beyond, but clearly understood this object, or one similar, has been here before.

My dream companions then encourage me to warn everyone, and with deep concern, I suddenly find myself calling out, "Look; this too, can happen to you!"

Following my next set of instructions, I turn my entire body to the right to face a large, unique picture window with no apparent supports; standing freely, out in the open. I am told this window is to be looked "into" rather than "through."

Adjusting my thinking process, I stare at what appears to be glass and watch an uncanny scene develop.

It is apparent that a dramatic change in the weather has taken place with everything frozen solid; all is white. At first, there is no sign of life. Then, vague images begin to emerge which are easily recognizable as people. All are garbed in white, but different shades of white, easily distinguishable from the frozen background. They stand silently, like statues, on this bleak stage.

Slowly, as though by command, they begin moving forward one at a time. It is like seeing history in reverse, from the not too distant past *backwards*. I recognize a dress worn by my grandmother. I see another from... was that the 13th century? Then another...Greece? Is that from Greece?

There are no faces to these people; only deep, dark voids; just like the eyes of the children I saw when my dream companion sent me into the city that was controlled by the Frightening Force.

As these people approach the actual window, each one in turn slowly fades from view as the next figure in this irregular line-up takes more definable shape and moves forward. Straining to get a better look, I cannot believe what is coming next!

There is an astronaut! An astronaut? I have no idea what an astronaut is doing in ancient history. I am thoroughly confused!

In the center, now, is a linen-robed figure with his back turned to me. I do not understand why his back is turned when none of the other's had been. He is dressed in the linen robes of the Christ's period, but based on the procession of figures, was MUCH older than that. Who is he?

In my eagerness to behold my Lord, I strain to see his face. He has not chosen to move forward in proper sequence as the others have done, but remains aloof and allows the others to pass him by and present themselves first.

Does this mean he has endured all histories; that he has existed during all ancient periods of man? I don't know.

Finally the linen-robed figure begins to turn around. I strain, again, to see as he advances in my direction. I wait, breathlessly, for the opportunity to see his face at long last.

But, with great horror, I quickly turn away, knowing that I do not want to see his face. I sense he is not the person I was looking for; he is not what he seems. This one is to be feared.

As I turn away in fright, I see another "ball" coming. This one is descending straight to Earth. As it hits, it gently bounces off Earth like a beach ball and travels out into space. It appears to be a replica of Earth, herself, with the same blue and green patterns as a globe. I see no particular features or other markings save the blue, where water should be, and green, where the land would be. This is not to say the water and land mass are in equal proportions as to what we know of Earth today.

In review of this dream, my companions tell me that a large object from outer space came close to hitting the Earth once before and caused at least one of our ice ages. I get the impression that it caused the orbit of the Earth to be changed significantly too, becoming more elliptical (oval).

Since the object was white, is it our moon? Did it get caught in our gravity as it attempted to pass us by?

I don't know. My dream companions did not say.

I do know, however, the other ball that was the color of the Earth, is a twin planet to this Earth. I have no idea how this can be, or where it is now. At some point in our distant past, I am told this "twin" came close enough to push us off our orbit around the sun and placed us in an lopsided, elliptical orbit whose one end brought us much close to the sun then the other.

We are being told that both of these events have the *potential* to happen again, in our Lifetime. That's all I know.

If the white object I saw was our moon, how can this same event happen again?

111

Easy! There is a lot of "stuff" traveling through our Universe and the Milky Way galaxy whose travels have not yet been plotted. At this time, we cannot state with confidence when an object will strike us. We just know it will. We could wind up with another moon or two, or the object could just pass us by; hopefully, with not enough gravitational pull to affect planet Earth.

As for the events that took place in the picture window, we are being shown that what is about to take place has happened many times before in the course of history for both man, and this planet; both the celestial events shown and the influence of the Frightening Force.

This evil force, or Frightening Force, has been around hounding mankind for countless ages. These years go back into a long, lost history of man; much further back then he is presently aware.

We say we are living in the Space Age, but *at least* one other Space Age existed in the distant past.

Who were they?

I have no idea. My companions did not say. To them, a specific time-frame or name is not important as they do not operate in a three-dimensional world that is bound by clocks, tides and seasons. They exist in a time/space warp that is quite bendable.

The scenery I witnessed through the picture window represents several ice ages, or polar shifts, which have taken place before. Each of these sudden freezes has dramatically altered the biosphere for inhabitants of the Earth; both flora and fauna, fish and fowl, and with even greater certainty, man himself.

In writing of these things, I am well aware that most conventional archeological evidence suggests that man has only experienced the most recent major glaciation (during the Pleistocene era), although several smaller pulses of glaciation occurred during that period also.

I am told to tell the people, "**Look, this too can happen to you!**" And, some of it will.

How much "white" we will have when we "shift?"

I do not know.

What areas will be affected the most by this "white?"

I don't know that either.

I do know that it will happen again, just as it has happened many times before.

I do not discount the possibility of white from a nuclear war, but I was not shown any evidence of explosive behavior and would have to conclude that this was not the message I was to give.

Again, as far as being affected by the objects that flew past our Earth; yes, they happened in the past; but, are once again a current potential; a possibility. It is not a certainty at this time. Man has the capability of changing, or modifying these predicted events.

The linen robed figure I first thought was the Christ, is the same soul who has plagued man since the beginning of man's arrival on planet Earth.

He is the Evil One, The Deceiver.

A few days after this dream, the Great Being, or **"THE FATHER"** introduced Himself. His displeasure over us is apparent and His words reverberated in my head as He shouted His warning:

Oh, Silly Nation of Ridiculous Souls! See you not the force of which I have warned? Know you not that the Prince of Darkness dwells here on earth? He is clothed in white and shall be heralded by many as the Second Coming. But heed him not for he is no son of the Most High. His fame shall be great, his miracles many, his deception unparalleled in human history. Of him you shall hear before long. Put no trust in Him or with Mine Angels you will never dwell. Hold sacred My Covenant with you and thou with Me. I AM THE FATHER, THERE IS NONE BESIDE ME.

~ THE FATHER ~

This is not the voice of the one who acts as a protector and big brother but a voice that commands special attention. He claims to be **THE FATHER** and states there is no other.

To be sure, we are being scolded and warned by a figure of great significance.

Hear Him well!

The Advocate called us foolish, told us our thoughts were rancid, and furthermore, we had no backbone. This was in regards to our seeming inability to stand up for truth and righteousness. Now **THE FATHER** is calling us "**silly**" and "**ridiculous**" based on our unwillingness to give ear to all the messengers He has sent to give us warning; both past and present.

THE FATHER has announced Himself to us out of exasperation. He cannot understand why we choose not to see what is taking place; how we totally ignore the horrible, evil force which is encamped around us. He has sent so many messengers to warn us for so many years and yet we still do not comprehend; we *will* not comprehend.

He asks us, "**See you not the force of which I have warned?**" He tells us that this "**Prince of Darkness**" lives here, right now, on planet Earth! We are told that he is dressed in "**white**," which is an indication that he parades as a "good guy."

We are also warned that many people will think he is "**the Second Coming**," but we better not be fooled because we have been warned.

Next **THE FATHER** states, "**heed him not**" as a reminder not to get drawn into anything this clever one gets started, as he does not belong to the kingdom in which our Father reigns.

We are told to be aware of deception; that his deception shall be "**unparalleled in human history**." We are cautioned to remember that if we willingly choose to "**trust**" and follow this sly one, we can forget about our chances of living with the angels.

When He speaks of "**My Covenant with you and thou with Me**," I must confess that He leaves me confused; and this must be for a deliberate purpose... to cause speculation... to cause us to question... to push us forward to find supreme knowledge that has been withheld.

I know only of covenants with the Jews and the Christians, and the mother of Ishmael. I'm afraid my knowledge is quite limited in this area. But, reason suggests to me there is much more.

If I have been called to be a "watchman" for these United States; for this America and her people, then the covenant must be with *this* nation.

I find this extraordinary!

In addition, He is obviously speaking of America because he addresses us as "**Silly Nation of Ridiculous Souls**." I cannot believe that all of a sudden the word "**Nation**" refers to mankind as a whole. The Advocate never indicated this to be so.

What agreement was made by our forefathers with the Great Spirit?

Has history recorded it somewhere?

How can we, the people of these United States comply with a covenant of which we have no knowledge? Somewhere, it must have been written down.

THE FATHER speaks again:

Hear me well, Obscure Nation; for your folly brings contempt to My throne. I spit on thee! My Son you proclaim with your mouths but they are empty words which drop like mist on the parched desert where no one but the Father knows that it did indeed exist. You say, 'But we are not an obscure nation. We are great among our brethren.' But I say, you are obscure; obscure to me! Your promises have been many; your actions few. My patience wanes. Your time is at hand.

~ THE FATHER ~

First, **THE FATHER** addresses us angrily, "**Hear me well, Obscure Nation.**" In His choice of the word "obscure" our Creator is making direct reference to the fact that we are "lacking or inadequately supplied with light"; His light.

He is stating that we have hidden ourselves in the dark and are covered with a veil so that no one knows who we really are.

"**Your folly brings contempt to My throne.**" In this statement He speaks of several topics in the one word "**folly.**" He is speaking of our lack of good sense and foresight, our lewd behavior, and worse than that, the foolish actions and criminal conduct by which we will bring about our eventual destruction.

He wants us to know our life on Earth is a serious matter. It is not appreciated that we are acting the role of the court jester.

No jesters are wanted.

By behaving in this manner, **THE FATHER** tells us we bring "**contempt**" to His throne; His Seat of Authority. In front of the whole world, we show no respect or reverence for the Great Being that we claim to honor. We set poor examples.

If we, who claim to believe in Him, willfully disobey His laws and His warnings, and show open disrespect, then the non-believers will mock Him and display their open disdain for both Him and His followers.

THE FATHER will be forced to take serious action to regain his authority over rebellious children.

Enraged, the Great One states, "**I spit on thee.**" This is not an American way of showing disgust, but this technique of spitting on the ground near someone, or actually on someone has been used for centuries in some countries as a clear indication that the person spit upon is considered to be of the lowest form.

Now He attacks the hypocritically, pious folks with His words, "**My Son you proclaim with your mouths but they are empty words...**" Here He is attacking all who claim the Son as their Savior, including men and women "of the cloth," who have no real connection with the Divine Son whatsoever; those who merely claim this relationship for prominence and stature within a community. These are individuals considered to be unworthy of **THE FATHER'S** attention and/or protection.

"**...which drop like mist on the parched desert where no one but the Father knows that it did exist.**" In this phrase, we are told that our words are so insincere that they never reach their destination. Our words are like a vapor that is entirely consumed by the scorched atmosphere surrounding a barren wasteland. The words are so hollow that they just evaporate into thin air where NO ONE knows they even existed; except **THE FATHER**.

These words of proclamation come from spiritually arid individuals, and **THE FATHER** states that only He is aware of our meager attempts and they are not worthy of His attention.

Now this Creator goes on to talk to us about our boastfulness. He claims that we do not believe we are an "**Obscure Nation**"; that we are in the dark without adequate light. We not only *think* that we are great, we actually *brag* about being "**great among our brethren.**"

As far as He is concerned we *are* obscure; obscure to Him.

He does not wish to look upon us.

We, as a nation, are reminded of our empty promises to all, including **THE FATHER**, when He announces: "**Your promises have been many; your actions few.**" Apparently, we have been making lots of commitments to suit our own needs, but failing to complete our end of the bargain. He cautions that His patience is dwindling when he says, **"My patience wanes."**

Like an earthly father who is reproaching an unruly child, He is telling us not to push Him too far. Our poor conduct, foul words and deeds, and lack of respect for higher authority will no longer be tolerated.

One day the many voices of warning will be silent.

We are told, **"Your time is at hand."**

Chapter 13

A NEW SONG TO SING

Autumn crept in on silent wings this year, with very little color change to stir the imagination. I don't know whether it was due to the abnormally dry summer or the prolonged warmth leading up to October's close; but, without the grandiose fanfare of brightly adorned leaves making their final exit, I felt somewhat cheated.

Autumn has always been my favorite time of year; a time when all of nature makes major preparations for the onslaught on Old Man Winter. I can look over my shelved food supplies and admire my canning handiwork that will take us through the cold hibernation period of a resting land with great satisfaction.

I am truly learning more about the edible weeds and wild things that I set out to accomplish in the not too distant past. They have been of great benefit to both me and my family. I shall continue my research and delight my taste buds with items not found in the local grocery store; items rich in good, old-fashion nutrition.

Some time ago, my unseen friends warned us of the need to save our grain (cereal). We were warned of a disaster that would strike this Nation of Plenty through flooding.

Much later, another warning was issued in regards to a dwindling food supply with a focus on more than just grain. Here is what I was shown:

DREAM... **In this particular drama, I was taken to a grocery where I was a participant in the existing chaos caused by knowledge that when the grocer's shelves were empty, there would be no more food.**

By the time I arrived on the scene, people were behaving in a crazed fashion, rushing about madly, pushing metal grocery carts wildly. They were snatching

food in all greed from shelves and even from one another's carts.

I found a cart of my own and began making my way through the panic-stricken mob, picking up a little of this and a little of that, snatching a couple of cabbages as I went. There was nothing else left in the vegetable bins and little else left on the shelves; certainly, no grain.

Finally making my way to a checker, I found that no one seemed to be "grabby" any longer. I felt as though I had entered some sort of "safety" zone; an invisible line of demarcation.

Standing in line, waiting my turn to be processed, I looked out through the enormous picture windows in the grocery store and noticed huge open-sided trucks on the asphalt parking lot.

These trucks were filled to capacity with a host of food and ready to roll; all that is, except one, which was neatly stacked with corn, tomatoes, beans, and melons. The trucker was carefully tossing on the last of the corn.

I began to cry, tears streaming down my face, as I watched the man close the gate on that last truck.

I sensed that when the last of the corn was loaded it will surely be the end.

I don't know why I felt that way, but The Advocate quickly began to explain that the tomatoes, beans and other nutritious foods, that were being loaded on the trucks and hauled away, were a clear representation of our spiritual and material riches; the end result of a nation under God.

They were being taken away.

The cabbages, he said, represent a purging.

It is to show us that there are those who sit in seats of authority within our own nation, who intend to rob us of our "nutrition," our "health," and our great "wealth"; to PURGE us of all we have.

I am told they weave this deliberate plot with kings, princes and leaders of other nations who wish to see us in defeat.

Not all those who occupy these seats of authority within our nation understand the full significance of what they are involved in. They too, are mere pawns in the game of chess that is being played for the life forces of these United States.

My unseen companions tell me that the corn is not symbolic. It is real and shows that the last of our wealth lies in corn; the only staple food left for our security. When we begin to ship out *large* quantities of our corn to other nations, for whatever reason, our death grows near. More corn needs to be held for the people of this land.

We are further told that our nation needs to be more careful concerning the sale of so much of its nutritional wealth to countries that cannot pay, and default on a regular basis. Someone has to pay, and it is has always been, traditionally, we, the people. This America does not have unlimited resources of grain and money.

Near the end, it will be a difficult decision-making process when both people and livestock compete for the same food in these perilous times. We will need to keep the animals fattened to provide us with food, but will not have the grain to feed them. We, ourselves, will need this corn for our own immediate survival; our own bodily survival, and future seed source. The choice, particularly with corn, will be whether the animals are fed, or whether the people are fed. There will not be enough to sustain both.

More grain houses must be built, and they need to be controlled locally. These grain bins cannot be federally controlled, or there will be nothing left for us; the people of this land. These storage buildings will need to be meticulously constructed to withstand *incredible* winds, and floods of the *worst* kind.

We are being told that our time is growing short and much individual preparation must be made. It is time for people to experiment with vegetable gardens if they have not done so in the past. A need to understand and correctly plant and harvest will be essential. If we do not know how to can, preserve and dry foods for storage, we need to learn quickly.

We should re-examine the weeds that grow in our yards, and in neighboring fields.

Are they edible?

How do we prepare them?

It is important for us to remember that these wild plants, we call weeds, sustained people for eons; long before the corporate grocery stores were in vogue. These hardy little plants have survived for multiple generations, and it is they, who will continue to survive when most other cultivated crops fail.

121

Our weather conditions will become more erratic, making the usual planting and harvesting seasons questionable, at best. To help ourselves through the changing times we need to store large quantities of food for each family member, taking into consideration their individual needs. Each of us could record pages of those items we deem essential for our own individual families.

Make those lists now.

Then, put your lists into action.

In addition, we might consider making arrangements to leave the cities when the streets become filled with madness from uncontrollable people, and reside where food can be grown as a family unit or community effort. If we can make advance arrangements with family or friends who live in the mountains, plains or deserts, to move in with them when these predicted times are upon us, we will have a definite advantage over our neighbor who has done nothing.

We are told to stay away from the coastlines and the nation's major river beds, and don't be downstream from a large dam, but do go where you are comfortable, keeping in mind that selective planning is paramount.

The times ahead are not going to be easy.

When the time of chaos in our biosphere arrives, we will gladly give up expensive material possessions, or large quantities of money, for something as simple as a gallon of fresh water.

Paper money will have no value.

We will not be able to depend on our grocery stores; the grocery store shelves will be empty!

Transportation will be at a near standstill.

The Advocate states that this once-great nation has been tried and found guilty.

Electricity will be non-existent, and without this useful energy we can forget about heated homes, running water, cook stoves, microwave ovens, toasters, TV, radio, hot water, and the list goes on.

Forget about all those files that were so carefully recorded in your computers; they're unretrievable.

We suddenly find another problem setting in... disease.

Without the ability to keep ourselves and our utensils clean, bacteria becomes one of our worst enemies.

The picture is not pretty.

I am not trying to scare anyone.

I just want us all to look at the facts and get prepared *today*.

It is my job to warn you!

We *do* have time; but again, we must act quickly and plan carefully, not in panic. Panic will only cause us to forget many of the critical supply items really important to our family's physical and spiritual survival.

Keep this fact in mind always: we DO have the opportunity to completely change and/or modify MANY of the scheduled disasters that are directly induced by our poor behavior. The Advocate told us so when he stated, **"If it were not true, I would have told you."**

I wonder how many disasters we can cancel if we really try?

And so, after the above review of "things about to go wrong," my dream companion sends me on another excursion to a place I've been before.

DREAM... **I am climbing a hill by myself. This is the same hill that my companion and I had been climbing previously when the police officer warned us that our lives were in danger.**

I have now, long since passed the point where he had originally stopped us and am almost at the top.

I see the tower and sense my companion is just around the corner waiting for me. This is the tower from which I must sing the "new song."

Suddenly, my companion and I are actually *in* the tower. I don't know how we got there, but find myself at the very top of this tower, in a room encased by glass windows overlooking the city below. This place reminds me of a small version of a flight tower.

I am standing in the middle of this tower room, facing the city below. It is night. There are very few lights to be seen within the city itself.

My companion tells me to move closer to the city, and as I do so, a microphone on a stand appears before me. This particular kind of microphone is familiar to me; I used it in the past when I used to sing.

**I hear music. I know that I am supposed to sing, BUT
I DON'T KNOW THE WORDS!**

**In a panic, I call to my companion, "But, how will I
know the words?"**

**As the music continues, my companion calmly replies,
"I will teach you."**

**Under his guidance and with a great deal of trust I
open my mouth to sing, having no idea how the words are
going to be given to me.**

**Suddenly, I hear my own lyrical voice in perfect
harmony with the beautiful music; words pouring forth.
He is giving me the words!**

**I know I must sing this new song "loudly." I must
project my voice. The people must be able to hear; I must
get the message to the people.**

**He has told me that my words are what the people will
need to hear in order to help them destroy the Frightening
Force.**

Well... after all this time, I have finally reached the tower to "sing"
my new song to the people.

When my dream companion told me he would "teach me a new
song to sing" I assumed he meant some new type of religious song.

How could I have known that it was not really a "song" that I was
to "sing"; not in the terms of singing notes on a musical scale? It was
actually "words" given to me by the Force that I was to excitedly relate
to others in celebration of a wondrous happening.

That wondrous happening was the fact that a Force far greater than
ourselves chose to come forth, make itself known, and provide us with
a chance to rectify our wrong doings.

It chose to show us exactly what was taking place within our
country so that we could not say, when judged, we did not know.

This Force has chosen to bestow on us a fighting chance to make
things right.

How could I have known that I was to utter words in musical tones
and with musical inflections and modulations within my own voice to
bring about excitement, hope and joy for those who would listen; all in
books co-authored by The Force.

My new "song" is to be found within the words contained in the book(s) I am to write.

When I asked him, "But, how will I know the words?" he answered most appropriately when he stated, "**I will teach you.**"

And he has.

My unseen companion will continue to give me the telepathic words necessary to act as warnings for this nation and her people. All those things I have been commanded to write and record will have to be "sung" (written) to America and her people to help them destroy the terrible forces which are in control.

So, I will continue to write.

I will act as a messenger on behalf of the Force, just as they have commanded.

I realized also, that reaching the tower was a task set for me from the very beginning when I was told, "**Son of man, I have made you a** *watchman* **for the house of Israel (America); whenever you hear a word from my mouth, you shall give them warning from me.**"

Mr. Webster describes a *watch-tower* as a tower for a lookout.

He defines a *lookout* as: 1) one engaged in keeping watch, and 2) an elevated place or structure affording a wide view for observation.

A *watchman* translates to be "one who keeps watch: a Guard."

In a way, that's kind of exciting.

If I am a pre-selected "watchman" for America I must be as observant as a Forest Ranger in a Fire Tower. I must keep my eyes open for "smoke," use my binoculars to get a better look, and relay any information I receive from the Force to the people of this land.

What fun!

Hear My words, Oh Weary Man. Sing My songs. You are not forgotten; ye of little faith.

~ THE FATHER ~

THE FATHER asks only that we hear (read and listen to) His words of Comfort and His words of Advice. He knows just how weary we have made ourselves by our improper actions and thought processes; how we have dirtied the library of our mind.

He invites us to sing His songs, the songs of love and praise, songs that bring peace and serenity. He wants us to forget about the ugly state in which we have lived for so long. He wants us to leave the past in the past, and make ourselves anew.

Some spring house cleaning of the mind and body, and a little remodeling will do just fine.

We are told that we are not forgotten, no matter how angry He gets with us and He wonders how we can have so little faith in Him as a responsible parent?

Chapter 14

THE LOWER KINGDOM

Hideous forces are encamped outside our physical, mental and spiritual doors everyday. They never go away. They patiently lay and wait for the opportune moment when they are granted entrance through our unprotected open doors. The trick is, not to let them in.

Gaining access to our physical body is quiet simple; they just hop on and cling to us. Yes, they actually take form so that they may be seen by those attuned to witness such materialization. Many of today's psychics frequently see them hanging on to people, especially in and around a hospital environment due to man's illnesses.

This in no way suggests that hospitals, in and of themselves are bad. On the contrary, they are critical to our survival. It only indicates that these manifestations thrive on the illnesses of man; his dis-ease with himself, others, and his own Creator.

Once we have departed from the hospital environment, if we ourselves are not negative, the creatures will leave us and "hop" onto some else. Or, they will continue to roam the hospital corridors looking for an opportunity to feed on a negative situation; thus, enforcing the atmosphere they love best.

We fight spiritual battles daily in an unmarked arena, and probably do not realize that these ugly forces are seated just outside that arena as an unwelcome audience where they cheer for the negative forces that battle us for our very souls.

In some respects, our mental attributes are not much different than those of the spiritual, with respect to the ugly, fighting forces. If either our mental or spiritual selves are not properly attuned to our physical body, and our Creator, illnesses of various form can move in and eventually conquer us. That is why we must remain alert, stay informed, and take the necessary action to correct whatever is ailing us with great haste.

My above analysis is not intended to move an audience to believe that this is the one and only manner in which mental illnesses occur. Not at all.

I know that many other factors can be deeply involved, but based on my own mission, I am addressing only that as it pertains to our spirituality.

Human emotion, as wonderful as it is, can cause us to act and react in such a manner as to be detrimental to our health. Often, the more undesirable of these emotions can cause us to engage in conflicts that otherwise would have been overlooked. When these particular negative emotions are produced, they emit a negative force field around our entire being on which the hideous force gleefully thrives.

At this point the ugly force is now in control and stays with us, cheering us on to create more and more negativity. It is only in a negative environment that these unwanted forces thrive, and the physical, mental and spiritual illnesses of man are their primary playgrounds.

If the negativity that surrounds you ceases, so do they. They will go elsewhere to survive. But, please keep in mind, our friends can bring these creatures into our homes also, and unwittingly leave them there. Hence, carefully selecting ones friends becomes a necessity for sustaining a healthy environment.

Keeping this undesirable force away from us is not as uncomplicated as it may seem; this must be clearly understood. When a door is left standing open, even if only ajar, the ugly forces can gain entry with ease. Our spiritual doors must be well guarded when open, and closed tightly when we are no longer on watch. The doors must be sealed tight when the destructive force seeks a new playground for enjoyment.

Hang out a "Not Welcome" sign and send them on their way.

Let me tell you about one of these creatures that played havoc with our family for *years*.

During those times, I could sense that something was wrong, very wrong; but just couldn't quite put my finger on the problem. My whole being was receiving the impression of some kind of invasion, but I could not identify it.

It was clearly in my house, though, and I had to play a waiting game, searching the corners of my mind for the smallest scrap of evidence in helping me identify the nature of this intrusion.

I tried to distract my own thinking processes by dwelling on everything from football games to canning, from new business products and customers, to shopping for Christmas presents, but it wasn't working. When I peered outside my living room windows even Dame Autumn, herself, seemed just as restless as the mood swings I perceived within the atmosphere of my home. And as a family... we were falling apart!

I begged The Force for help in identifying the cause of unrest that was creating so much havoc in my home. The Force replied with a vision in the hopes of assisting me. This is what I was told:

VISION... **I think I have been grocery shopping, although that really doesn't matter. I am returning home in my station wagon and my daughter, Winni, is in the car with me on the passenger's side. I am entering our circular, gravel driveway and I can see that the front door is ajar. I think that rather odd. I know I closed it when we left.**

I see Twinkle Toes, the family dog, madly scratching herself as usual in the driveway, seemingly unconcerned. Silently, an eerie pall creeps over me as I sense that something is *most* wrong. Very wrong!

Now I am suddenly very angry and frightened, all at the same time. I gather my wits about me, step on the gas pedal, and drive straight across the grassy circle that lies in the center of the driveway, deliberately heading straight towards the open door.

Honking my horn constantly, as I drive across the grass. I want to make sure that whoever or *whatever* is inside my house knows that I am acutely aware of its presence!

Terror strikes me as I realize that this *THING* might well destroy me if I were to enter.

Slamming on the brakes, I come to an abrupt halt in front of the brick retaining wall, gravel flying everywhere. I then turn on the car headlights and direct the beams at the partially open door. In fierce panic, I flash the lights on and off several times while still honking the horn. I want to make *sure* this *THING* knows that *I* know it exists!

Still greatly frightened, I back up, turn the car around, and speed away; again, gravel flying in every direction; I must get help!

I make a left-hand turn from the driveway onto the main road and nearly run into an officer in his squad car. I toot my horn several times anxiously, to attract his attention, and pull up along side him as he slows down to a full stop.

I am near hysteria at this point and frantically roll down the car window in all haste so that I can tell him of my problem. But as I begin to speak to him, I realize that *NO ONE* will be able to help me. *No one* will understand. No one, save me alone!

The frightening vision did provide me with my answer; a severe spiritual warning for my family; one that I pray never happens to you, the reader.

At the time of this vision, I did not wish to acknowledge what my mind already knew. I preferred to ignore the warning, just a little while longer.

I was in no way prepared to deal with this new danger at all.

This threat to my household had nothing to do with the catastrophic Earth changes that were to happen on land and sea. This dealt strictly with the "principalities" that invade our lives and attempt to destroy our families, and our very souls.

These creatures are not too numerous now, but will come in *droves* in the near future. We need to make all the preparations we can to ward them off *BEFORE* they gather momentum.

This one entered our home when we left our spiritual door ajar; we failed to keep watch and he just walked right in.

I don't know how he did that, but it doesn't take much for them to gain entry.

I wish I could say he forced his way in, that he *pushed* the door open himself, but I don't think so! I did not leave my front door open when I left to go shopping, but apparently I did not close it securely, either.

A few days after this vision, I felt that my mother and I might have been the culprit in creating this abnormality. She had been so unhappy when she arrived for her visit, and we fought almost continuously during her stay. I thought the two of us may have created some kind of negative energy force; but, I now know, that was not the case.

IT caused us to fight!

In the beginning, this creature could not be physically touched nor could he be seen. But that changed.

His existence threatened the beauty of my once peaceful abode, and I cried day in and day out when no one was around. I was sick with fear and helplessness. There was no one who could help me!

This destructive force had grown stronger and stronger since I first noticed it nearly six months earlier.

How was I to defeat it?

How was I to defend myself?

How was I to protect my household?

One morning, as I came downstairs to prepare breakfast for the children, I turned to walk into the living room en route to the kitchen; often taking this route to view my lovely backyard and majestic mountains.

However, in mid-stride, I was forcibly blocked from entry into this room by a protective force, bringing me to an abrupt halt. Fear immediately seized me as I realized that something *hideous* was in my living room!

I must not enter!

I could not see it, but I *KNEW* it was there.

Stunned, I immediately withdrew my foot and froze in the front entrance way not knowing what to do.

I needed to think!

After a moment's pause, shocked, scared and dumbfounded, I hastily retreated in another direction. Still running, I raced through the kitchen and breakfast room to a swinging door that separated the dining room from where I was currently positioned in the breakfast room. This was the only other way the "thing" could reach me on this side of the house.

I made a grab for the door and pulled it closed!

My only thought now, was that this "thing" was sealed off; it *wouldn't* enter my kitchen area.

I have no idea why I felt safe behind a closed door; however, I quite honestly believe it had something to do with what my mother had once told me about a healing ceremony performed by her German grandmother.

As a young woman, Mother was suffering extensively due to a harsh reaction from a smallpox vaccination. A puss sac, the size of a baseball hung from the underside of her arm causing much fever and pain.

Her grandmother, who was visiting this country at the time, stated she would perform a "cure," but while conducting this specified procedure, absolute silence would be imperative.

Mother watched with great interest as her father's mother performed a calculated routine whereby she deliberately walked in and out a doorway several times, slamming the door with each entrance and exit. Mother said the whole process, including prayers, lasted some twenty minutes.

Upon completion of the "healing" ritual, my paternal great-grandmother explained to Mother that the opening and closing of doors was necessary to banish evil spirits.

Within less than one hour's time of concluding this rite, the swollen arm showed noticeable improvement and by morning, the swelling, pain and fever were gone.

A violent reaction to smallpox was certainly not my problem; but, I reasoned, if a closed door could help Mom, maybe it would help me!

I stood there for a moment trying to think, but that was impossible. I was so shocked I could barely function.

Minimally collecting myself, I found fixing breakfast to be quite a chore; I could not clearly focus on the issues at hand. Each child had their own special needs which required proper handling in order to get their day off to a comfortable and happy start, and I was less than coherent as the family threw questions at me while making preparations for their day's activities.

No one seemed to notice my stupor.

I would not let the children exit the house for school by way of the front door that day, and they could not understand why.

I can't begin to remember what I used for an excuse, but it took a lot of urging on my part to keep them away from that area.

The children left for school, and all that day I felt the terrible presence in my home. It seemed to move from place to place, and was much stronger in some areas than others. I had no idea what was happening. I didn't understand it at all. I said nothing to anyone. The next day, the same thing occurred. It was still in the living room!

My fright was slightly less than it had been the previous morning, but I detoured the living room, anyway.

My unseen friends had clearly delivered me from the grasp of evil the day before when I was totally unaware of the dangers that lay in front of me; but, now that I knew how to perceive this foe, they did not need to interfere. No protective, unseen hands needed to save me from this horrible force this morning.

Who was this unwelcome visitor?

Was this the presence that my vision had warned me about?

I think so.

Was this real, or was this a part of my imagination?

I had to conclude, based on help from my unseen friends, that this was clearly not the fanciful notions of an unstable mind.

This was real!

It could have injured me.

Still... I said nothing to anyone.

On the third day, I WAS MAD!

I marched into the living room right to the chair where this "monster" was sitting. Seeing a vague outline of his form I pointed my finger at him, boldly announcing, "You can't have me! I belong to God!"

I turned my back on him in defiance, and walked straight through the living room, dining room and breakfast room to the kitchen.

I was so angry I was on the verge of tears!

My dander was up!

How dare this "thing" enter my house and scare me!

How *dare* he cause chaos and charge up negative vibrations in my family and my home.

I was *NOT* going to tolerate this kind of energy form; this despicable new enemy. *HE HAD TO GO!*

I tried everything I could think of to rid my home of this terrible beast. But as the weeks went by, the ugly force became so strong that I finally had to gather my three youngest children together and tell them about the focus of negative energy that almost had form.

I explained that each time they were openly hostile to one another, this "thing" became stronger, causing even more chaos in our home.

Fortunately, our eldest son was away at college and did not have to contend with such adversity. I was not about to bother this pragmatic son with tales of unidentifiable "spooks" and things that go "bump" in the night. It was not necessary and would have caused him much unrest to know of such conditions existing at home.

I bought each of the younger children a gold cross to wear on a chain around their necks at *all times* while in the house, and requested that they work exceptionally hard at being super nice to one another in order to help destroy this would-be creature.

With carefully chosen words, I explained to the children how this "creature" was actually being "fed" by their negativity.

Whenever the children fought, or my husband hurled angry words at the children or me, the hideous force grew in strength. It gained real form; I could physically see it. With each passing day, it's appearance became more and more detailed as harsh words were carelessly tossed to the four winds.

Conversely, when the atmosphere within the house was peaceful and harmonious, this force diminished in physical form and intensity; it seemed to fade.

I decided that the hideousness of this monster must be crushed. I walked the boundaries of our property and pleaded for the legions of the Most High to guard well the frail edges of my tiny kingdom and protect all who entered. I begged that no evil be allowed to seep through. I traced every door, window and fireplace with my own hands. I placed love in every possible corner, yet could not destroy the monster who dwelt within.

What greater power would I have to find within myself to destroy the blackness?

Fear gripped me as I realized that my own life forces were being drained from me. I was afraid of becoming too weak and therefore, unable to provide protection for my family.

I was absolutely beside myself; my family was in a state of near collapse. They seemed sickly and lacked strength. They were lost somewhere in time.

Love that was so abundant to all within the framework of this house was almost totally destroyed by the fanciful workings of tortured minds. Even my husband was rarely home. I feared we were drifting apart.

I could hardly function. My movements were animated and my thinking lacked continuity. It seemed centuries ago that I last took pen in hand to write.

The original idea of me being a part-time secretary for my husband's business had long since been adjusted. Business had increased, and I now had a secretary of my own.

Continuing to work in our business office was difficult at best. It took so much strength to think, send out proposals, talk on the phone with customers, check on orders and make "cold" calls, that each night I fell into bed in a state of pure exhaustion. At one point, I even submitted a letter of resignation to my husband.

Our desks faced one another, and after reading my notice, he made an "airplane" out of my letter and "sailed" it back to my desk.

"Resignation denied," he smiled as the "airplane" came to an abrupt halt in my lap.

He had obviously not taken me seriously.

I could plainly see the matter would have to be discussed in significant detail later.

Our son, David phoned from college one afternoon to say he would be coming home for a few days. His father had been traveling a great deal recently and Dave (as he now preferred to be called) thought he should come home and see if his mom, sisters and brother needed any help.

I was grateful for his thoughtfulness. I was so tired. I needed a rest from this battlefield where I was attempting to slay the monster who walked the halls of my home. I felt Dave's presence could possibly help me regain some of what I had lost. He was strong, and had been away from the house for a while, so I felt he would be "safe" during his short stay with us.

No gold cross would be necessary for his protection.

It was late when he arrived that evening, so we talked very little, deciding to save our news for more alert minds come morning.

Dave chose to sleep on the family room hide-a-bed, having voluntarily given up his bedroom to his youngest sister when he went off to college. This family room shared a large fireplace with the living room although it was not a "see through" situation. The open hide-a-bed covered the entire area in front of the brick fireplace with just enough room to comfortably walk in and out of the arched doorway leading back into the living room.

Sleep was sound for me that night, but rather fitful for Dave, as it turns out.

In the morning, I fixed a simple breakfast for the younger children and sent them off to school as usual.

Dave slept on.

Not wishing to wake him, I completed my upstairs morning chores, then headed for the kitchen for some hot tea.

As I descended the stairs, I paused when I heard Dave call me. Responding, I passed through the living room towards the family room where he had spent the night.

I asked, "Did you sleep well?"

He stated frankly, "Well, quite honestly, no! Mother, what is in this house?" he questioned with genuine concern.

"What do you mean?" I asked with an attempt to conceal knowledge of his insinuation. I had told him nothing and I knew his siblings had not either. They were asleep when he had arrived the night before.

"There's something in this house!" he stated with some alarm.

"Its presence was so thick last night that I nearly got out of bed to shake its hand and introduce myself: 'Hi, I'm Dave.'"

"Mother, what is it?"

Upon further investigative conversation, I learned that he sensed this presence beside the hide-a-bed, in front of the family room fireplace. It was through that same wall, in the living room, where I had been most frequently encountering this creature.

I took a deep breath, let out a big sigh, and began to relate the painful story of this creature and the incredible negative energy levels that resided within this home.

We talked about his dad's unhappiness and apparent hostilities. We discussed the continuous squabbling and outbreaks of anger among his siblings. We discussed the individual hardships perceived by his sister, Pam.

It was nice for me to know someone else felt the unwanted presence and the power of its being; its very existence.

It was good to have someone to share my fears with.

Finally, I had someone who understood!

Dave hesitated about going back to college, but I assured him everything would be fine.

After he left, I thought long and hard about our conversations and decided to go to the minister of our church. I reasoned that as a Man of the Cloth, and a graduate scholar of one of our theological institutions, he *MUST* know about these things.

Surely, he could help; after all, our churches constantly warn us about evil, and this *thing* was the epitome of evil!

I gathered all my courage and gave the church a call.

Having thus made an appointment to meet with the leader of our church, I arrived at his office and began my tale. I told him everything I knew about the recent happenings and the hideous force.

When I finally stopped talking, I leaned back in my chair and awaited his wise council.

Silence reigned for an inordinate amount of time.

I was confused by the delay in his response, but pleased when he finally began to speak.

"Have you seen (the movie) The Exorcist?"

My heart fell to the floor.

He was referring to the current movie of that same name whose story follows the life of a young girl possessed by the devil.

I was momentarily paralyzed by his insinuation!

By his question, and the look on his face, I knew that he thought my imagination had been influenced by that movie.

I didn't bother to tell him that I had *NOT* seen it, had no intentions of seeing it, and that our "creature" had been around a lot longer then that dumb movie!

Silently, with my heart in my throat, I rose from my chair, thanked him for his time and left.

He simply said, "It was nice to see you."

I couldn't believe it!

Still in a mild state of shock, I found it a long walk to my car from his office, even though it was a mere twenty-five feet from the door to the edge of the curb.

This Man of God had no clue as to what I was talking about. My realities were in no way a part of his thinking, his teachings, or his reality. I had just learned *that* bitter lesson!

The creature continued to play havoc with my family for months and months; sometimes appearing just outside one of the children's bedroom doors.

I never told them.

He apparently did not care for laughter, joy or any positive, light-giving energies, and on these days stayed away. His presence was non-existent.

My husband came home less and less and when he did the creature that we all had reasonably subdued would be reactivated. I wanted so badly to tell Johnny, but I dared not.

Sometimes I knew the creature was actually ON him; on his right shoulder.

I dared not say a thing; he would never have believed me.

One night, right after Johnny left on another business trip, I finished watching television and went upstairs to bed.

At the entrance to our bedroom, I was startled to look across this huge room and see the creature in *full form* sitting on the edge of our bed!

He had picked up enough negative energies that I was able to see every detail of his ugly, hairy, ape-like body.

His legs dangled over the side of the bed as he sat there looking at me; his legs being too short to allow his oversized feet to touch the floor. His dark brown hair fully covered his body and was fairly long, although not disproportionate to his height, which I estimated to be some four (4) feet, not including his ears.

The moderately pointed ears stood on the top of his head, similar to that of a dog, and were well positioned and proportionately designed for his overall appearance.

His hands seemed no different than those of a monkey and he had considerably more hair on the front of him, from his chest to the lower region of his body, than that of an ape or monkey.

The shape of his head was more rounded than oval and it was difficult to identify the features on his face due to so much hair. The eyes appeared dark brown or black and were difficult to see for the same reason as my inability to clearly define facial features. There was no evidence of protruding, leathery lips; they simply could not be seen.

When he stood, his posture was slumped like an ape and his exceptionally long arms hung down to approximately mid-calf.

He had been sitting on Johnny's side of the bed and, at the sight of me, began sliding off the bed heading towards the adjoining room where we maintained our business office.

I was *infuriated!*

How *dare* he be on my bed!

How *dare* he occupy my husband's side of the bed!

I screamed at him as I lunged through the doorway with full intent to *KILL* it; kill, with my bare hands!

I did not know whether I would live or die, and I really didn't care.

I had had enough!

He was destroying my home!

The creature turned and looked at me, somewhat surprised, as I rushed towards him.

I don't know what happened next.

I don't remember. I just know that all of a sudden I found myself lying down on the bed in my usual place.

I was afraid to move.

With rapid eye movement, I scanned my surroundings looking to the left and straight in front of me.

I could not bring myself to look straight up, or to the right where I had last seen the ape-like creature.

I quickly leaped to my feet, throwing my legs over the left side of the bed, and hurried out of the bedroom, into the hallway.

There I stopped, turned around, and timidly looked back into the bedroom in the approximate area where I had last seen the creature.

He was gone.

I turned on every light in the upstairs hall, office and bedroom.

I was so frightened I wanted to cry, but there was no one to comfort me.

Sometime later, I spoke to a friend, Dr. Cecil Springfield, about this matter. He was a noted clinical psychologist of whose professionalism I was well acquainted. Cecil had served as senior psychologist at Denver General Hospital from 1964 to 1966 and chief psychologist at the Federal Youth Center in Littleton from 1966 to 1969. He also was a member of the clinical faculty at the University of Colorado Medical Center, a consultant to Denver Children's Home, a field instructor at Fort Logan Psychiatric Hospital and a lecturer at the University of Wyoming.

Dr. Springfield was also a leader in civil rights activities and was one of the founders of the Malcolm X Center for Mental Health.

We had first met in 1976 while working together on a project called PROGRAM HEALTH, developed and implemented by renowned health and fitness expert, Debbie Drake, in which state-of-the-art plans were coordinated for a life-long health maintenance regime; including diet, biofeedback, specialized exercise and behavior modification.

Later, Cecil had assisted Johnny and I with our educationally learning disabled child, and also provided marriage counseling for the two of us at a time when hopes for reconciliation were still high.

Fully trusting him, I told my story and gave a detailed description of the "other world" creature.

"Why, Nancy," he responded, "there's a whole book on these creatures in the Denver Public Library. You ought to read it. It describes many of these creatures, including drawings and a description of what problems they are known to have caused. It tells all about them."

Thank God! I was finally believed! It was so nice to know that I had not lost my mind.

There really was someone else besides my children, who understood, and backed me.

Long after Cecil provided me with the knowledge as to where I might possibly find information pertaining to this creature, I did visit the Denver Library. Here, I searched for the recommended book both myself and with the aid of a library assistant; but to no avail.

Failing in my efforts to locate this recommended reading, I called a mutual friend to inquire where I might find Cecil these days, since I knew he had retired. I needed the title to the book, if he could remember it.

Sadly, she informed me Cecil had passed away from cancer some years earlier giving me to know, I was on my own in this continued research. My options were coming to a fast close.

I had not yet exhausted my possibilities and tried several of the larger libraries in the surrounding counties without success. I was rather disappointed not to find this rare material as the information could have been most enlightening for me and of wide service to others.

I will continue my search in this area.

The creature did fade considerably after my "attack" on him, but still, he did not completely go away. His presence remained in the house for a long, long time where he continued to wreak havoc on us day after weary day.

I share this strange story in an attempt to show you that *MUCH* is about to take place in the very near future.

These *ARE* the times which were spoken of more than 2000 years ago. There will be all manner of things with which to cope. These are the "principalities" of which we have been warned.

We can store food to eat, burn wood to keep warm, boil water for safe drinking and endure many hardships, but how do we fight hideous forces we have never before encountered?

How do we survive attacks of entities whose existence is denied by all too many of our religious leaders?

Talk! Communicate with one another! Carefully select *TRUE* friends. Seek out those who *DO* understand.

Do not be afraid to speak of your experiences to others as they may need to hear the stories for confirmation and support of their own happenings.

It is imperative that we stand together; if divided, we will fall (fail).

Chapter 15

REMEMBER JONAH

Our fight was long and hard; seven whole years!

We fought with everything we had, and our losses were heavy.

The "creature" that dominated our lives for so long was *VERY* real. I sometimes feel that he won, but I refuse to accept that.

In any case, we are now a divided family. Our peace, tranquility and innocence was destroyed long ago.

Johnny and I were divorced; our house sold. As Winni and I packed up the last of our material possessions and drove out the circular gravel driveway for the last time, we never even looked back. We prayed we were leaving the creature behind. We prayed he would not follow us to our new home.

I purchased a country home in the foothills where Winni (now 15) and I were its only human occupants among a backdrop of richly, towering old cottonwoods and pines.

Winni was the only child left at home; everyone else was gone.

Johnny and I had owned two small companies that predominantly served the medical profession and in the divorce settlement, I received one company; he took the other. I eventually moved the business, in its entirety, to my new home nestled in the back corner of a pie-shaped, five-acre lot.

It was peaceful there.

A wonderful little creek meandered through the trees at the bottom of the hill where a thick rope was attached to a huge old cottonwood tree, tempting passing humans to swing across the chilly waters. The rope would swing its occupant like Tarzan from the shoreline, over the creek and back again.

I was no Tarzan and had no ambition for the role of Jane; so, this pleasant pastime was left in the hands of Winni, her friends and neighboring children.

Somewhere in the midst of all these trials, and after Pam had graduated from high school, she spoke to us of her desire for a name change. She felt that her christened name did not suit her; she just didn't feel like a "Pamela." She liked the name "Bobbi," instead.

With some reluctance, we accepted her wishes and tried to adjust to this newly chosen name as proclaimed by court decree.

My life had been in turmoil for too long and I was having some difficulty organizing "Nancy." I prayed that all would work out well for Winni and me, and found comfort only in reading books and attending church on Sunday mornings.

On one such Sunday morning, my mind had wandered off on its own course pondering the age old biblical statement of "mansions within a house." I was looking for new avenues to explore along these lines, when I heard the dramatic voice of our minister inquire, "How big is your God?"

I snapped back to present reality, once again an alert member of this fine gathering known as ROCKY MOUNTAIN CHRISTIAN SINGLES. We did not have our own church building at the time, but were delighted to come together on Sunday mornings, assembling in a large bar and dance hall.

(No! Nothing was served from the bar.)

Lively sermons were often given by our leader, who we fondly referred to as "Charlie" and this morning, Charlie asked his faithful throng, "How big is your God?"

What a question!

Actually I had never thought of God in dimensional proportions; but, why not? As I mildly began examining my own perceptions I was also listening to the laughter of this evangelistic following as Charlie gave hand signals to qualify "how big" some of us may feel this Great One is.

I thank Charlie for that question, as it has remained with me these many moons, and when I feel very small and lost in this enormous world of complex existence, I look to the skies and remember that I am a protected, tiny spark created by the omnipresent Original Fire.

With a Father *THAT BIG*, what is there to fear?

With a Creator *THAT BIG* there must be billions and billions of "mansions" to explore before my life on this planet ends.

My schooling was in session, once again, and so was my new life.

Previously, due to being unhappy, I had slammed shut the doors of my mind, bolted the entrance and marked it "NO ADMITTANCE."

I had no desire to hear any sacred messages; pay attention to any dreams; or think about any commitment to write.

I just wanted to be left alone.

I needed time to re-build "Nancy" and did not wish to be disturbed.

My childish actions did not go unnoticed, of course, and one evening my "poor attitude" was brought into focus by my unseen companions who presented me with a statement:

I am astonished that you are so quickly deserting him who called you... (Galatians 1:6)

No mistake about it, I was in the doghouse.

It was obvious my sulking would not be tolerated and that I had better get my head screwed on straight!

I suppose I was behaving like a "Jonah"; I was trying to run away and hide. There was no whale to gobble me up for abandonment of my task, but it was crystal clear that I was being admonished for temporary desertion.

I was to get my act together and get back on the job.

I had work to do!

Just as the prophet Jonah was assigned the task of speaking to the people of Nineveh, I, too, had an assignment. I was to warn the people of America, and present the same alternatives to them; the choice being simple: change your ways, or be destroyed.

I was guilty of turning my back on the Force that had always been so gracious to me. I had made a non-verbal commitment to write and record; to take the messages and warnings, in whatever format, to the Force's intended audience.

I had promised to write down my directed experiences so people could open their eyes to the fabulous wonders around them everyday. It was imperative that the original command be fulfilled and I was neglecting my unwritten contract.

Remember Jonah.

~ THE FATHER ~

In the past, **THE FATHER** had mentioned "Jonah" to me and warned that this nation should "Remember Jonah."

Most people know the name "Jonah" only as the man who was swallowed by a "great fish" (some use the word "whale") because he tried to run away from God. He ran because he did not wish to deliver a message to the fierce kingdom of Nineveh and therefore, tried to hide from the all-knowing Creator.

It didn't work, of course.

So, how much more do people actually know?

Let me explain why **THE FATHER** has asked that we "Remember Jonah."

Jonah became a prophet when he was called by God to "Arise, go to Nineveh, that great city, and cry against it; for their wickedness has come up before me."

But Jonah had no desire to go there nor to speak to its people, and therefore ran away. He found a ship that was about to set sail, paid his fare, and boarded her in order to flee to another land.

A great storm arose at sea and the sailors feared for their lives. They prayed to each of their gods to save them, and threw much of the cargo overboard to ease the burden of their vessel which was threatening to break up.

When the captain found Jonah asleep in the inner part of the ship, he said to him, "What do you mean, you sleeper? Arise, call upon your god! Perhaps the god will give a thought to us, that we do not perish."

Meanwhile, the sailors had been casting lots to determine who was the cause of this great evil that had befallen them. The lot fell on Jonah. The sailors inquired, "Tell us, on whose account this evil has come upon us? What is your occupation? And whence do you come? What is your country? And of what people are you?"

Jonah told them that he was Hebrew and that he was running away from "the Lord, the God of Heaven, who made the sea and the dry land." As the sea began to rage with even more violence, Jonah suggested to the men that they throw him into the sea to free them from the Lord's wrath. They did so, begging the God of Jonah not to condemn them for taking his life. The storm subsided.

Jonah was swallowed by a great fish and remained in its belly for three days and nights until he was vomited out on dry land.

Now, God came to Jonah a second time and said, "Arise, go to Nineveh, that great city, and proclaim to it the message that I tell you." And this time he obeyed.

Having gone to the city of Nineveh, he issued the proclamation to the people as given to him by God, "Yet forty days, and Nineveh shall be overthrown!"

Jonah awaited the destruction.

However, the King of Nineveh believed the message that Jonah delivered because he had heard of the God of the Hebrews. Knowing that this was a great and kind God, the King removed his robe, covered himself with sackcloth, and sat in ashes to show his repentance (a common practice for religious apology). He made a proclamation and published it throughout his entire kingdom:

"By the decree of the king and his nobles: Let neither man nor beast, herd nor flock, taste anything; let them not feed, or drink water, but let man and beast be covered with sackcloth, and let them cry mightily to God; yea, let every one turn from his evil way and from the violence which is in his hands. Who knows, God may yet repent and turn from his fierce anger, so that we perish not?"

When God saw that the people in the great city of Nineveh were truly sorry for all they had done, he abandoned his plan to destroy them.

This change in plans caused Jonah to be exceedingly upset! He complained to God about it. He ranted and raved saying, "This is exactly what I thought you'd do, Lord, when I was there in my own country and you first told me to come here. That's why I ran away. I knew you were a gracious God, merciful, slow to get angry, and full of kindness; I knew how easily you could cancel your plans for destroying these people."

"Please kill me, Lord; I'd rather be dead than alive when nothing that I told them happens."

God then answered Jonah with a question, "Is it right to be angry about this?"

Jonah went outside the city and set up a leafy shelter where he sat and sulked! He had told this great city that it was going to be destroyed in "forty days," just like he was told to do; but they repented. God forgave them of everything they had done wrong, and withdrew His plans of destruction. Now Jonah felt totally humiliated because nothing was going to happen after all! He felt he had been made to look foolish.

Jonah still *wanted* to see the city destroyed! He wasn't worried about its salvation. And just in case God changed His mind, he now had a good seat on the east side of town where he would have a pretty good view.

The story goes on, but **THE FATHER** is most interested in having us focus on that portion which deals directly with the changing attitude of the peoples in the great city of Nineveh.

Now, Jonah had told them that they would be destroyed in "forty days"; the number forty actually being only symbolic in Hebrew, as many other numbers in the Bible are. Forty, represented "a sufficient time in which to get the job done." Therefore, no specific man-made calendar was being used to calculate when the destructive forces would arrive; God would decide.

The same applies to this nation and her people. We are only asked to show sincerity; true repentance and the same kindness will be shown to us.

We have the same opportunity to make drastic changes each and every time we are warned. No calculation by man will determine when the destructive forces will arrive. We will be given the same "forty days" that everyone else has been afforded. Everything will take place in the Creator's own timing.

None of us can run away from what we are supposed to do when a Higher Power is in charge. Just like when I was a youngster, playing hide-and-seek, I knew the only hiding I was doing was from my human friends; the Presence always knew where I was and what I was doing. An attempt to hide from a force greater than ourselves will only cause us more trouble.

I firmly believe that the prophets and soothsayers of today, that see these upcoming events, have a responsibility *to the people*. They must not act like a "Jonah" either. They must not go outside of the city and set up a "booth" to sit back and watch the destruction; to see how it will be done. They must work *with* the people to assist them in bringing about the necessary changes to benefit Mother Earth and the creatures that dwell thereon.

We also need to know that the God of the Hebrews, the One God for all humanity, will *always* give us warning before disaster beckons with icy fingers; but, know that warning has been given. Corrective measures must be taken so that our "parent" does not have to carry out His punitive measures.

148

The Universal Force has warned individuals such as King Solomon, King David, and hordes of other humans to change their ways over millennia. He has even warned nations to change.

It is no different today. That same loving Father is still around; still trying to get us to get our act together.

But, **THE FATHER** is stating most emphatically that He has reached His tolerance level. He is promising that He will unleash the anger that has been building up inside Him due to the delinquency of the souls He created. These souls that chose human form have acted no differently throughout the ages.

Even the Christian's Bible states, "It is known what man is."

We act and react the same over and over again.

For us to play the role of poor, misguided souls and demonstrate lack of respect and concern for the Great Authority, who is our parent, will no longer be tolerated. It is expected that we should have gained maturity through our many lessons in reincarnated lives; to have put away our childish things. It is expected that we will strive to become a responsible companion to He Who Is, Was and Always will be.

The Advocate understands that much information that should have been provided to us for our growth, has been withheld; but, we are being told that this excuse will no longer be accepted. We must step forward and take charge of our individual lives and the life of our nation.

He understands that it is difficult for us to advance in our schoolhouse on Earth when the learning tools have been withdrawn, but asks that we not dwell on this matter, and simply concentrate on making the major changes in our lives that will bring us in full accord with **THE FATHER**.

Some years ago, there was a Game Show on television called, "Truth or Consequences." The games were fun with much laughter for both the participants and the viewing audience.

Right now, this country is participating in another game of "Truth or Consequences", but there is no laughter.

God is our Host.

Remember Jonah?

Chapter 16

MAKE HASTE

There is a famed story teller whose name we know as Aesop. This Greek slave is said to have lived around 600 B.C. and told fables meant to teach morals and offer useful advice. One of his most popular fables is The Ant and the Grasshopper.

In this tale we find the Grasshopper hopping about chirping and singing to its heart's content one fine summer day. An Ant passed by, hauling an ear of corn, with great difficulty, to the nest.

"Stop and chat with me," the Grasshopper coaxed, "instead of working so hard. The weather is pleasant and we have so much time."

"I cannot, for I am helping to put away food for the winter," replied the Ant, "and highly recommend you do the same."

"Why should I bother about winter?" laughed the Grasshopper, "we have plenty of food at present."

But the Ant continued on its way and slacked not in its task. When the winter came the Grasshopper had no food, and found itself dying of hunger, while it saw the ants distributing their storehouse of corn and grain which they had collected during the summer. The Grasshopper watched with sad remorse and regretted that he had not taken the Ant's advice to prepare for the days of necessity.

As in the story of these creatures, now is the late summer of our lives; time to prepare for the days of necessity. We still have time to gather in our own bounty, both physical and spiritual; time to provide for ourselves and be counted when the "harvest" is drawn in.

I speak, and you hear me not! I weep, and you turn your heads! Time creepeth upon you like a slithering snake, yet you continue to play your childish games and not store up your Heavenly treasures. Wicked, wicked man who lives in a desert of bleached bones and human decay, where has

**thy stinking thoughts and foul deeds led thee? Thy Father
looks on thee in disgust and vomits as He views thy record!**

~ THE FATHER ~

The first sentence spoken by **THE FATHER** hardly needs
comment:
"I speak, and you hear me not!" He speaks, and we do not listen.

Within the second sentence lies a real tragedy: **"I weep, and you
turn your heads!"**

Think about that... would you really turn your head, pay no heed,
and walk away if you caused your dad to cry?

Wouldn't you comfort him, give him a hug, and tell him you are
sorry?

Wouldn't you try to make things right?

When our Holy FATHER is in tears over His misbehaving children,
we actually *TURN AWAY* from him; we have no pity, no empathy, no
compassion.

The Advocate has explained to me that in bringing us into existence,
THE FATHER had been looking forward to companionship with
entities who would share with Him in all the joy of His creations. But we
have turned our backs on Him; He is *lonely*. We just don't seem to care.
We are selfishly preoccupied with gratifying our own wishes and taking
advantage of "the good life," as we see it. We are having a great time
playing games on planet Earth; games that may well hurt us in the end.

But we don't care.

Guess we're still in that party mood!

As for the beginning of the third sentence, **"Time creepeth upon you
like a slithering snake,"** having witnessed the swift, sleek and silent
movements of the snake, we can easily equate the passing of time with
the illustration this treacherous fellow. Many times the snake's swift and
silent moves go completely unnoticed by man as he works and plays in
his own self-created environment. In his failure to broaden the horizons
of his self-induced, minuscule world, man has failed to see the obvious.
More pointedly, man *will not* see the obvious.

So, in this manner, time is eluding us right now.

Further, he tells us, the inhabitants of America, that even though we see the "slithering snake" and know that Time is running out, we continue to "**play your childish games and not store up your Heavenly treasures.**"

In making use of the word "**play**," our Wise Parent means we are behaving frivolously, moving aimlessly about, and mocking Him. We are acting like children with no regard for the consequences of our behavior.

The term "**childish games**" refers to the *simplemindedness* with which we approach this *contest* for our very souls and our precious land. We conduct ourselves in a ridiculous fashion, always expecting that **THE FATHER** will bail us out.

We do not store up our spiritual treasure; fortify and nourish it... our concerns are too materialistic, we are told. Money and the things that money can buy are of greater consideration. We are not striving to rebuild our spirits and return them to their original completeness; a true shame since the spirit endures forever. Our bodies are only temporary housing while living on planet Earth.

Benjamin Franklin had a lovely party to commemorate his eightieth birthday, and is reported to have had a delightful short conversation with one of his guests.

The guest, upon greeting Benjamin at his front door, inquired, "So, how is Benjamin?"

Benjamin replied, "Oh, Benjamin is just fine, but I fear the house he dwells in is tumbling down and he may soon have to vacate."

It would appear that our forefather had a better concept of which was the more important ingredient in the existence of Mankind; the soul.

Next He addresses us as "**Wicked, wicked Man...**" which needs no explanation, and he goes on to say, "**who lives in a desert of bleached bones and human decay.**"

THE FATHER of Man desires us to know that *WE* have created a "desolate" environment for ourselves in which He finds no vitality or good health in us. We can't stand up; this Nation and her People have lost their strength. We have collapsed into a pile of bones that have no color; no hint of vitality. Our basic structure is all "dried up"; we are worthless; and *this* is the environment in which we have chosen to live.

This **"decay"** He refers to is our "corruption." He sees us as being "putrefied." We have created a foul environment, are deathly ill, stinky and decomposing rapidly.

And to further this tirade, he wants to know, **"where has thy stinking thoughts and foul deeds led thee?"**

Almost to the bottomless pit, I would say.

After all we have done to ourselves, our foreign neighbors and our nation, have we bettered our lives, our country, and our well-being through our foulness?

The answer is obviously and emphatically, "No."

"Thy Father looks on thee in disgust and vomits as He views thy record," we are told.

We know the word **"disgust,"** and **"vomits"** is a pretty strong choice in word association to indicate His displeasure. But, we can plainly see that as He reviews *His* historical records of us, and our nation, it makes Him sick enough to puke!

To hang our heads in shame is not enough. To don sack cloth and ashes and feign remorse will not cut it. The sands of time in the hourglass of man have all been used up. No longer will our misdeeds be ignored.

In this same session from which I received the above message from **THE FATHER**, The Advocate stepped in to play the role for which he is so aptly named. He wishes us to know that our Creator really *is* crying. He wishes us to know that even though our Father has expressed his anger towards us, He still loves us.

> **Tiny creature of small significance in this vast universe, know that Thy Father loves thee! He weeps and grasps tightly His stomach for His pain and agony are great. He, with broken heart, calls His children Home. Hear Him. Find Him. Follow Him. There only is Peace.**
>
> **- The Advocate**

We are but a speck within the tremendousness of this great universe, and even though we are **"of small significance"** our Father loves us.

And, we, the love of His Life, have broken His heart. He is still calling us, begging us to come home.

Surely we all can relate to the pain caused by rejection. How often, as human beings, have we been totally crushed when someone else has rejected us, and by that rejection, we know that the other person simply does not care what happens to us or how we feel?

We are told that it is no different for the Great Spirit.

The Advocate pleads for our weary Father: "**Hear Him. Find Him. Follow Him. There only is Peace.**"

After hearing this heart-wrenching, mediation speech from The Advocate, indicating the Mighty One's great agony and His love for us, I caution you not to take this lightly. There is only one more speech in which "tears" are referenced. After that, neither **THE FATHER** nor The Advocate ever speak of tears again.

I will tell you why later, after that last speech.

Remember in an earlier dream, when I was trying to warn the People to save their cereal, to save their grain?

Remember that no one wanted to listen; that they were too busy with the fun times of life?

Remember the fable about The Ant and the Grasshopper?

I think its time to decline any more invitations to the game of "charades" and leave the party. It's time to go home and clean house.

THE FATHER has repeatedly given or sent the same message over and over again to His people; spirituality needs drastic improvement. This message has been for the whole world of believers, to keep them on their toes; but, right now, He is more worried about this America, her leaders and her inhabitants.

We have been told by **THE FATHER** that our spiritual side is so lacking that He, He personally, will bring about these chaotic events. All the preparedness in the world will not help us if we fail in the one thing He states is mandatory; renewed spirituality; oneness with He, Himself.

Oh, Man, Man! I gave you my Son; Mine only Son and you believed Him not. I raised you up out of nothingness that your habitat would not be the slime of the world, but to the slime you have returned. The teeth of My fallen

angel glisten and gleam in direct defiance of My Will; for
his now seems the will of Man. I have been a constant
Father to My Creation; yet you heed not my warnings.
You, America, are nearly dead, dead to me. *Your* covenant
with Me has been broken, yet I have never once left your
side.

~ **THE FATHER** ~

After **THE FATHER** wearily addresses man, His oration discusses
the Son who he specifically sent to us as the perfect example of how we
should conduct ourselves as members of the human race; physically,
mentally and spiritually.

That Son, He declares, was "**Mine only Son,**" and we "**believed
Him not.**"

That Son was the entity we have come to know as Jesus of
Nazareth; that soul who took on human form and became the Christ.

When **THE FATHER** states "**I raised you up out of nothingness
that your habitat would not be the slime of the world,**" He refers to
the very substances of which we are made and where these substances
came from. He refers to the body that houses man's soul; the flesh and
bones that make up the form given to the species known as "Homo
sapiens." **THE FATHER** reveals to us that when He molded mankind
He chose the elements of Mother Earth. He chose soft, moist Earth or
clay. He was the potter, and we, the finished product of His making.

Upon completion of the species that would ultimately be called
human beings, He did not leave us to slither and dwell in the viscous
material from which we were made. He did not leave us to live among
the lower forms of life, such as algae, snakes, lizards, frogs, salamanders,
etc. Instead, He gave man a special place on this planet. He gave man
dominion over all the other species, both plant and animal. We became
the co-rulers on this terrestrial ball; standing beside **THE FATHER**.

Now He says of His deep disappointment, "**but to the slime you
have returned.**" He feels that we have totally fragmented ourselves so
that we have reduced our being to mere viscous mud. This viscous mud
is both slippery and slimy... a perfect home for frogs and a fine nursery
for algae... but certainly not the majestic level He had intended for man.

The next statement is really quite sad. Our Father now speaks of one of the Heavenly Host, a specific soul He brought into the universe to share all his creations. But, this soul defied **THE FATHER** and throughout eons of time has wreaked havoc on the simple minds of mankind, who were given free will.

THE FATHER states, **"The teeth of My fallen angel glisten and gleam in direct defiance of My will; for his now seems the will of Man."**

Like a battered parent, He wearily points out that the evil one is smiling at the chaos he has created, and thoroughly enjoying it. No longer do we willingly follow the advice and counsel of the Great One. We are totally captivated by the ugliness of the evil one, and have almost unanimously elected him our new parent. The grief of the Almighty One is most evident.

"I have been a constant Father to My Creation; yet you heed not my warnings," our Great Spirit moans. He is baffled as to why we continue to behave in this manner when He has been the perfect parent.

Now, filled with remorse, He angrily states, **"You, America, are nearly dead, dead to me."** This is a threat *AND* a promise directed at this land and its inhabitants, who are hanging on by a thin thread, as far as our Creator is concerned.

In His statement: *"Your* **covenant with Me has been broken, yet I have never once left your side,"** it is clear that we did not keep our part of the bargain.

But, *WHAT* bargain?

Who, in this world, representing this nation, had the right or the authority to strike such an agreement?

That's a lot of power... and the *second* time that **THE FATHER** references this covenant!

When **THE FATHER** originally mentioned this covenant, he referred to it as "sacred," which denotes the document (or verbal agreement) to be entitled to reverence and respect. In other words, it is "holy," to be set aside for special service... service to **THE FATHER.**

As I said before: "What agreement was made by our forefathers with the Great Spirit?"

Has history recorded it somewhere?

Or... is it recent?

How can we, the people of these United States comply with a covenant of which we have no knowledge?

157

Somewhere, it must be written down.
Someone must have intimate knowledge of this transaction.
Please come forth... help us; whoever you are.

After **THE FATHER** finished with the above speech, He did not go away. I could sense His presence and did not understand why He had not withdrawn.

I waited, ever ready to serve Him; waited in silence for what seemed to be a very long time.

I could not leave, because He had not left.

Why was He still there?

Then I sensed a vibratory change, like a sigh, and He began to speak in a more hushed tone; but, nonetheless, tearfully.

Oh, Child of Misery! Why do you treat yourself thus? Know you not that your Father grieves? Have the Heavens not rumbled enough for you to behold Mine tears? Look about you hastily, but see every nook and cranny, for the Evil One dwells on earth!

~ THE FATHER ~

"**Oh, Child of Misery!**" He calls out wearily. "**Why do you treat yourself thus? Know you not that your Father grieves?**"

He refers to us as a "**Child of Misery**" to emphasize our state of suffering. He knows that it is we, who have caused our own unhappiness and emotional distress through lack of Oneness with the Universal Force.

He asks us bluntly, "Why do you do this to yourselves?"

When we could have perfect health, no death, peace, harmony, love, beauty, etc., He cannot fathom why we continue to treat ourselves in such a retched manner; deliberately denying ourselves all the riches that are inherently ours as eternal spiritual beings.

He goes on to ask, "**Have the Heavens not rumbled enough for you to behold Mine tears?**"

The Advocate has told me that when man was first granted the privilege of residing on this planet, all the violent storms, necessary for its creation, had ceased. This newly formed environment provided a lush, semi-tropical to tropical atmosphere where a soft mist occurred at regular intervals to maintain the vegetation in a virtual paradise. It was into this stage setting that man was introduced.

After arrival, man didn't behave himself very well, making some poor choices, and taking undue advantage of the "free will" so generously given to him by his Creator. This free will then, became a negative tool in the hands of man through which he separated himself from the Universal Force. Through his juvenile thinking, man became self-assured that **THE FATHER** of all creation would never desert him; would always pamper and spoil him; provide him his every need; thus, maintaining his Paradise on Earth.

Not so!

All of this was true, for a while. Then one day **THE FATHER** put his foot down and said, "Enough!"

THE FATHER speaks for the last time in reference to His grief, His tears, when His states:

I will weep no more!

~ THE FATHER ~

His statement in no way implies we have finally found the path to spirituality. On the contrary, He is telling us that he refuses to waste His energies on us. As He stated before: **"You, America, are nearly dead, dead to Me,"** and He will not continue to grieve for a nation and its children when they are unresponsive.

This particular heavenly grieving and rage has nothing whatsoever to do with the normal process of re-birth and new creations that occur at an ongoing basis for the Earth Mother, but they *can* and will be used as "tools" by which to discipline unruly children and/or destroy an undesirable creation.

Let me depart, for a moment, from the explanation of **THE FATHER**'s message and take you on another "voyage" with me; far out beyond our solar system. This journey takes me back so far in time that I have no knowledge of bodily form. I want to show how we existed in pure innocence before our fall from grace; how we lived with **THE FATHER** in perfect harmony.

In this "voyage," I am obviously a young soul with no experience in the matters of disassociation with the Creator.

Oneness is all I know.

In describing the vision, I will use terms which are familiar to all of us today; yet, it would please me if you were to keep in mind that while actually taking part in this vision, terms such as: solar system, galaxy, Earth, planet, celestial, mist, beam, etc., meant absolutely nothing to me.

I saw all things through the eyes of an innocent spirit whose hand was securely held by the only Father she knew. I felt loved, honored, secure, unrestricted; and sensed no needs or wants. Everything I might have wished for was already provided.

I could use the words "pure joy," to describe my existence, but even these words cannot begin to ascribe to the ecstasy of my being.

When I began my approach to this planet I thought I was coming to "play"... something I frequently did throughout all of creation... but this time, lessons were being taught that interrupted my enjoyment. I was shown what happens when dis-harmony interacts with Oneness and causes chaos; disrupting the once peaceful co-existence of creative collectiveness.

VISION... **I am somewhere way, way far out in space heading towards a solar system. I believe I am in our galaxy and traveling rapidly towards a lighted area that is encircled by some type of enormous "light ring," which I sense is the outer ring to our solar system. I don't know what the ring is made of.**

My movement is effortless; there is no wind; although I know I am moving rapidly. Speed is only a word here, having no real value to describe my rapid progression. My only perspective of travel is in the observance of objects in the distance coming ever closer. The situation presents no fear. Time and space have no dimension to my awareness.

All around me is the deep, deep blue of space, almost black. I see no stars. The only light is coming from the solitary group of stars and planets contained within the approaching "ring."

I have no sensation of either heat or cold, I am comfortable with whoever or whatever I am.

160

Each aggregation of celestial bodies bound by the attraction of their chosen sun has always been a wonder to me; and as I pass through this immense ring, I recognize that this is a new star system in my circle of possible "playgrounds."

Equal in beauty to the others; yet fascinating in its own uniqueness, I pass through this ring acknowledging a wisp of air as though briefly touched by wind. Once through the ring this sensation ceases.

As I pass the many planets contained within this ring, I know that they are not of importance for this moment in my existence. My destination is the little, pale blue one.

I have stopped traveling now and am MANY miles above this planet I know to be Earth. I am directed to look at her, and upon looking, see some kind of covering that completely engulfs her so that I cannot see the Earth, herself. This covering is something like a glass bowl, a canopy, dome or rigid, circular veil that enwraps her. I can plainly see through the encircling dome to detect an undulating mist or gas of some sort which lies beneath.

Suddenly, I find myself *under* the covering where it is pleasant and this new "playground" is covered in large-leafed green plants, and huge flowers of every imaginable color. I seem to want to turn my face upward toward the underside of this rigid veil, and upon doing so, am bathed in something similar to a soft mist, but I sense no water. This "mist" does not remain on the surface of my skin because I have no skin. I am in a "spirit" body.

This "mist" is wonderful to experience and hard to describe. It is more like an energy form that is feeding me, caressing me and fulfilling every possible desire I could have, although I have no thoughts of "desire." The energy "mist" radiates down from the canopy above me, and as I float, absorbing the tiny droplets, I role over and over is pure ecstasy.

The "mist" is quite spectacular in itself. It consists of microscopic, golden particles that sparkle profusely as they slowly "sprinkle" to their destination. With the slowness in which they fall, I presume them to be extremely light in weight; everything being relative since I am not a human being.

I know that I am loved by a Force greater than myself, and that It will care for my every need. The energy particles are Its light intermingled with the watery vapors, that are nourishing me on this Earth. I am *with* the Force; the Force and I are united, our thinking is in one accord. There is *nothing* I want, absolutely everything is provided. I don't even have any concept of "want" or "need."

Without prior warning, I find myself now back at my original observation station many miles above the Earth, and watch as the pale blue covering over the Earth slowly disintegrates, exposing an entirely different Earth than the one I knew. My "playground" is totally exposed to all that surrounds it.

This new Earth; having lost her "newness" and purity seems to display more harsh features and deeper, darker coloring. Much time has past and she is much more "experienced" than when I first knew her.

A beam of particles is bombarded toward the Earth from somewhere far out in space. I know them to be an energy beam. Sometimes the beam goes into the Earth, and at other times it pauses on the Earth's surface. Then again, a beam may go no further than the area above the Earth where the outer most part of the dome once existed.

As the beam withdraws, great disturbances occur in the area where the beam had been focused, and there are rippling effects (repercussions) elsewhere due to the area originally affected by that beam.

Since I am so far above the Earth, all things created by that beam do not affect me emotionally. I do not recognize myself as having any attachment to this planet called Earth.

I am aware of Great Winds, not unlike the winds I have encountered elsewhere, but these Earth winds, I know to be of such magnitude as to be devastating to the beings that dwell on that tiny planet during this time in Earth's history.

In addition, I see tiny fires and know that these are volcanoes. Still, I feel no attachment to the beings that reside on this place, and am fully aware that the Earth, herself (her personage, her spirit) is not unaffected by what is taking place. However, she will survive and grow most beautiful with age; she will continue to exist.

On the other hand, I recognize that the Force is having to take action to modify a non-conformity.

We, are that non-conformity.

The Advocate explains that when the Mighty One is unhappy, *GREAT* disturbances are generated and thereby, emitted from His Being. It is like a reverberation, an energy field that creates and multiplies; that is, it creates something, that creates something else, that creates something even more, and so forth... kind of a "snowball" effect.

These energy fields are totally controlled by the Great Power, Himself. He can carry out His original plan, modify it, or bring it to an abrupt halt. It is His choice as to what He will do and when; it is a part of His continuous creative efforts; no thing remains stagnant.

But, I might suggest here, that "ill-will" towards man would not be a good thing, considering His magnificent power.

It is interesting to note, that while I was under the dome, I *did not* have a sense of *belonging* to the Earth. I only belonged to the Light whose force penetrated my being from the canopy above. The Earth was beautiful, but hardly noticeable to me as my delight was with the Light. The Earth was provided as a lovely playground for me, where I had no responsibilities. The Light took care of everything. I suspect that I was being shown that this is the way it used to be in the very beginning of our existence. Currently, we are a long way away from that perfect relationship.

Until rather recently, the plan of the Force was for almost total annihilation of the human species through an object being hurled at us from space. The plan has been changed; modified. The object is still on its way, but it will not strike us; not this time. We, like Nineveh, have been reconsidered; we are still found "wanting," but our execution is no longer imminent.

We still have the opportunity to provide the Great Spirit with further reasons as to why we should not be treated so harshly; why He should modify more of His plans; but that would take significant changes; the choice is ours!

Now... going back to **THE FATHER**'s words before I related the incidence of seeing Earth in her innocence, we are further warned, "**Look about you hastily, but see every nook and cranny; for the evil one dwells on earth.**"

He makes an urgent request. He begs us to keep constant watch: peek into every hole, lift every rock; seek out the evil one and do not be caught unprepared. That soul we refer to as Satan is alive and well, and living on planet Earth!

❉   ❉   ❉   ❉

Many years ago (1974), in the dead of night, a late October storm caught my family off guard. We were rudely awakened by the violent tossing of large hailstones on our brick home at the whimsy of Mother Nature.

So violent was her throw that my youngest son hurled himself out of his top bunk, certain that the stones would crash through his bedroom window and spread glass all over him and his bed.

The girls jumped out of bed too, and came running upstairs to seek out their parents as a measure of security. We all gathered rather nervously in the upstairs hallway where we knew we would be safe from any possible flying glass. We listened to the roar above as the hailstones pounded the roof. The noise was deafening; like a freight train rumbling only a few feet away, causing us to shout at one another in order to be heard.

Something furry brushed against our legs; it was Twinkle Toes, the family dog. She had readily abandoned her watchful station in the utility room, and with some degree of sheepishness, nestled nervously among the legs of those humans she knew would protect her.

Late October was extremely rare for producing hail storms in Denver, Colorado; but, by the following day after breakfast, little else was said on radio and television about the year's third violent hailstorm.

We searched the yard for evidence of damage and found little; except for the poor pine trees.

Examination of the outside walls to the house proved them to sustain only minor damage; but then again, they were brick.

However, the roof and north side of the house around the windows, was another story.

HUGE chunks of putty were missing from the casement windows, and innumerable pieces of roofing shingles were scattered all around the base of the house and strewn out into the yard.

This late in autumn there was little to destroy in the gardens. Squash, beans, corn, tomatoes, cucumbers, eggplant, etc., had been the victims of relentless anger twice before, never fully recovering.

I mention this incident only because of another dream dealing with stones hurled from angry skies.

DREAM... Seated on our living room couch, I am jarred by the sound of a terrible thud on the roof. It shakes the entire brick house!

"What in Heaven's name is that?" I hear myself ask as I leap up from my resting place and race towards the family room picture window, envisioning a more panoramic view of the problem.

Momentarily glancing out of the huge living room picture window as I race by, I fail to catch a glimpse of whatever hit my roof.

I see nothing!

Reaching the family room window, I gaze in a southerly direction and see an enormous hailstone crash to the Earth. This hailstone is followed by many others of its kind; but, the strangeness of the sight is in the spacing and size of these destructive cannon balls from Mother Nature.

These hail stones from the darkened skies are spaced so far apart that in the beginning, my head darts to and fro as I watch them descend on the fields around me. As they begin to rain down with greater speed, the quantity of hailstones increases greatly, also. Their size is most impressive, appearing to be about the size of a tetherball or, perhaps a bit smaller... being some 7"- 8" in *diameter*. I gasp in horror, wondering if any of these monstrous bundles of frozen moisture will strike the house again, and dread the thought of one coming through the plate glass windows.

Storms of this magnitude are scheduled in the near future. The Advocate comments on this dream and states his concerns in a less-than-calm voice.

I have warned and warned! Do you hear or does my message continue to fall on deaf ears? Know you not the consequences of such a storm? Can you not imagine the miserable deaths of agony for man and beast dealt by these stones cast from Heaven? Fools are you to believe Nature is out of control for God remains at the helm.

- The Advocate

In case man had some sort of notion that nature was out of control, The Advocate reminds us that God is very much in command. He stands as Captain of All That Is, and Ruler of the Universe.

The Force warns that these are serious matters. When "**these stones cast from Heaven**" begin to fall with greater frequency, intensity and size, the damage will be beyond belief! Insurance companies will *not* be able to cover the losses, and our government's disaster relief funds will be all dried up!

As we rolled into the 1990's, it was reported in the Rural Electric Nebraskan Magazine that hailstones measuring four inches in diameter fell on the Nebraska prairie, killing livestock and smashing homes, barns, chicken coops, etc. The county in which this took place offered 4% loans in order to help the farmers and ranchers get back on their feet.

The time is not far off when even loans for repairs will not be available. The disasters will come in such rapid succession that recovery will be impossible: recovery from political disaster, economic chaos or unprecedented weather anomalies.

All of you have heard elaborate predictions concerning the eventualities surrounding the multiple changes in California, but I have a new one for you.

Come with my friends and me as we go to San Francisco Bay somewhere in the not-to-distant future where a breathtaking event is about to occur.

DREAM... I am in the air over San Francisco Bay and stationed well above Alcatraz Island on the eastern most end. My eyes are drawn westward; out past the Golden Gate Bridge, which is a bright orangish-red in comparison to all other surrounding colors.

Something is on the horizon, but I can't quite make it out. I watch intensely as the mass grows darker and larger.

I am aware that as I am watching this mass grow in the Pacific, no one else knows about it, they have no idea what is coming.

I am told to look around, where I see all manner of boats in the bay, happily going about their routine of business and pleasure. I look at the tall buildings and housing stacked high on the rolling hills. I have no emotional feelings for anything except the little sailboats that dot this watery scene. They bring me a sense of peace.

Being mildly distracted by all that I have been observing, my unseen friends request me to re-focus westward, once again. In doing so, I am faced with a dark mass growing in the ocean, and know EXACTLY what it is... a *TSUNAMI!*

As the realization strikes me, the giant wave rolls over the top of the Golden Gate Bridge, crushing it as though it were made out thin metal pieces from an Erector set. The wave surges forth slamming into the buildings high on the hill to my left, leaving them to crumble as though made of sand and straw.

The tsunami advances well inland before it begins to retract its mighty claws. In its retreating path to the sea it takes all manner of debris with it; including people.

I heard no noise as I watched. It was as though I was inside some type of soundproof enclosure; but the sight of that giant wave will long be remembered.

And so it goes... we are continuously provided with warnings of the future which come in the form of words or picture excerpts from a Force

that has declared Its everlasting and devoted love for humankind; a Force that extends well beyond this realm. Each presentation is given in hopes that we will be shaken enough to take positive, corrective action.

Will we?

Chapter 17

DARKNESS COMES SWIFTLY

Night has once again extended her hand to me and I have accepted her gracious offer to rest and await another day. As I slide under the covers and bid the day a fond farewell, I close my eyes and envision a beautiful spot on a mountain hillside where I often go just before sleep engulfs me.

The veil of darkness quickly overtakes me providing quiet rest until dawn graciously makes its subtle entrance. All too soon I find myself awakening to sense a smile on my face brought on by some external process. I mildly acknowledge that night has gently passed and find myself pleasantly absorbing warmth from the early morning sunlight as it cascades through my east-facing windows.

The open bedroom door leading to the redwood deck, ushers in a cool breeze that causes me to snuggle down among the covers once again. I hear the cheerful sounds of water droplets coursing the twisted, pebbled path of the tiny creek just a short distance away. Feathered friends serenade the new day and lull me back to sleep as I slowly disappear into another world.

DREAM... I am standing outside on my redwood deck with friends. The sun's rays are so warm that they make me sleepy. I am peacefully observing the beauty of the azure blue skies and listening to the melodious songs of Madam Spring's mating birds.

Suddenly, an eerie feeling creeps over me, and as this occurs, the birds cease their spirited tunes. The beautiful blue sky turns rapidly into night with no companion stars to keep her company; no moon to light the way. One by one, in rapid succession, the lights for man disappear.

I stand in eerie silence awaiting some dreadful event.

171

In a broad sense, there are many ways to explain this dream, but they all portray the same event. Put quite simply, the Age of Man, as we know it, is about to end. We are among a cast of players participating in a long running theatrical performance called "Life."

Through reincarnation, we volunteered for each and every role and are responsible for its ultimate success. Our performance has been poor; the curtain is being drawn; the lights turned out.

As children of the Most High, we originally bathed in spirituality and spiritual truths, and were rewarded well by our Father. There was an openness about us and we shared everything; we were a delight to be around, and in turn, we enjoyed everything around us.

We had free will then too, but we were so attuned to the Great Force that it never once occurred to us to act outside Its will. We were content to be in harmony with All That Is.

But, something went wrong; very wrong. Something happened to interfere with that relationship. We no longer walked and talked spiritual truths, and sadly, even lost the meaning of many. Our openness with others was almost non-existent and we began to find less and less enjoyment in the beauty around us. Our behavior steadily declined and our rewards diminished proportionately.

The Creator sent troops to the little planet called Earth to act as advisors on matters of spiritual behavior. He sent His angels, prophets and soothsayers, the Masters, His Son, and even put in a special call to some of his children that still might be able to hear. He commissioned these troops to speak to His children on His behalf and deliver messages of warning; providing them the opportunity to make major adjustments.

He was, and still is, asking that we seriously consider making those major changes now or, He will make them for us!

He does not like to threaten His offspring, but we have left Him little option. He is a weary Parent.

If we do not change, He is warning that He will take everything away; all that He has provided so generously in the past, and we will have to start all over again; from "rock bottom."

If He must carry out His threat, He will leave no lights by which to guide man's steps. When the lights go out and darkness reigns, then we will feel the full force of His fiery. The "curtain is being drawn," "the shade is being pulled" on the last act in the life of mankind.

The Force feels that this America and her people, the whole world in fact, are living in darkness based on their separation from their Creator; their very source of light.

The word "darkness," simply translated, makes reference to that which is "devoid or partially devoid of light." We use the term in a variety of forms, such as someone's "dark side"; behavior that is negative and moody; perhaps, even scary or violent, or we may use the term to describe something evil, threatening, dismal, foreboding, morbid, sinister, cloudy, murky, etc.

A "dark" day for a nation might be when someone of great importance dies or we are plunged into war.

On that fateful day in 1929, (known as "Black Thursday"), when the Stock Market crashed, I have no doubt many considered it a "dark" moment for our economy.

Another "dark" day occurred in the life of this nation when the Supreme Court ruled in favor of Madelyn O'Hare, among others, to strike prayer from the Public School System in the late 1960's; prayers offered in honor of the God we claim to serve.

After years of thriving, Europe found herself plunged into a form of darkness, better known to us as the Dark Ages, where much knowledge, schooling, artistic and technical skills were lost.

The WORLD BOOK Encyclopedia records this period as approximately the 400's - 900's A.D. in which the early centuries of the Middle Ages witnessed civilization sink very low in Western Europe. Knowledge from ancient Rome survived only in a few monastery, cathedral, and palace schools. Knowledge acquired by the Greeks nearly disappeared. Few people received schooling. Many ancient artistic and technical skills were lost, and in their ignorance, writers of the day accepted and recorded popular stories and rumors as *truths*.

Now, you might wonder why I choose to step forth and briefly discuss a period of time wrapped up in darkness, which appears to have no bearing on America and its inhabitants?

I do this to show a marked decline in the forward progress of the human race.

This comment may well be argued, but I respectfully submit that I am not criticizing our wonderful scientific and technological advances;

they are great and much appreciated. This comment is made only in connection with the many messages I have been asked to present to the people of America; presented to warn them that many truths are being withheld causing them to remain in the position of uneducated children.

Materialistically, we're running a fantastic race; but, spiritually we haven't even left the starting gate.

Based on the above analysis, we might even refer to our present living as the "New Dark Ages"; this being selectively determined by information which is continually withheld from us as well as the misinformation and disinformation with which we are spoon fed.

We are not exactly going backwards; yet, without truth there is a marked decline in the forward progress of the human race.

Think about it!

In this highly computerized, technological society, of which we are members, I would expect that we should have truth in all areas of our existence, and believe our mental and spiritual advancement depends on these truths. We cannot remain "children" forever; we must be allowed to grow.

Whether the subject matter is: political misconduct, economical deceit, entities from other planets (aliens), or world shattering finds that cause us to rewrite the history of the human race or force us to rewrite our religious doctrines; we need to know.

I might add, here, that in accepting many of the new ideas, or truths, our minds are due for some pretty healthy shocks. The adjustments will not be easy. We may not like what we hear and see; but, it is far better to know these facts then continue to live in a world fraught with absolute lies; creative fiction and hidden realities.

I am going to take this whole scenario one step further and discuss a disturbing aspect of our existing economy. Although the scene may look grim, it has the potential to produce a magnificent, positive ending.

Again, I must remind you, I did not solicit the information. The Advocate presented this information based on his concern for the state of this union between America and her people, and requested that I warn you.

The Advocate and his companions explain that we are living with a false sense of security based on our monetary system and materialistic desires. Our economy is no more stable than a house made of cards, irregardless of what we have been told. Our monetary system has been so cleverly manipulated that when we begin to fall, we will fall HARD and FAST! Here is what I was shown:

DREAM... **I have just entered a very large room with extremely high ceilings. The room reminds me of Grand Central Station in Washington, D.C. as it existed during World War II. This huge room lays within a building which is old and stately while the room itself, is ornately decorated with white marble, trimmed in richly colored dark wood, and boasts highly polished counters of wood and marble. I am under the impression that this was constructed sometime around the late 1800's to early 1900's.**

The counters are located in the center of the room in a circular fashion and are handsomely carved, circular counters with frosted glass sections mounted on the top. They remind me of the old bank buildings I visited while accompanying my grandmother to her bank many, many years ago.

Venturing half-way across the room towards the circular counters, to gain a better vantage point, I stop and look around me. I believe this room, maybe even the building itself, was built long ago to be used precisely for the very purpose under which it is currently operating. The floor appears to be made out of marble, and the sounds of customer's clicking heels echo continuously as they traverse the huge expanse in order to conduct some type of business.

I do not see any women; the clicking heels are surprisingly, from the shoes of men.

I am here to purchase shares of something. I have not yet decided shares of what and begin walking nonchalantly towards the counter. As I am approaching the counter, I hear some low voices of disenchantment. These rapidly

gain momentum until many voices can be heard shouting with hostile disapproval. As the shouting continues, papers are being frantically waved by clutched fists. The customers seem very angry. The Handlers behind the counters seem unconcerned.

I do not see any of these Handlers out in the lobby area with the rest of us. They stand behind the counters where they are safe from the angry patrons. Becoming curious as to how these people are able to get in behind that massive counter, I slowly begin an investigative walk around the counter perimeter searching for some sort of swinging gate which permits these Handlers to enter and exit. I do not find a gate, but DO find an opening which startles me.

Peering inside this enclosure I see that these men are standing on narrow, slightly elevated platforms that are attached to the circular counter. They are standing on their toes in order to remain on this platform and not fall off.

In the center is a black hole. I mean, the whole, entire area is a void! These Handlers are taking the papers from the angry customers and tossing them into this great nothingness.

I am suddenly made to realize that all of these customers are throwing their monies into something that has no value; there is nothing to back up the investment. They are not real! Everything is on paper only. If the customer ever tried to collect his monies, he would sadly find that there had never been anything of real value to purchase in the first place.

As we see in the dream, the Handlers are standing on a ledge around the inside of the counters, which means two things here: 1) that they are allowing the customers to "buy on a margin"; and 2) that they, themselves, are balancing precariously on a ledge in the hopes of not falling into "oblivion"; they want (not need) the money.

We are told that they are standing on their toes in order to remain on this elevated ledge (platform) and not fall off. (At this point, the word platform takes on a new meaning.)

The Advocate explains that there is an elite group handling (the Handlers) many of our stocks and they have created for themselves a narrow, elevated "platform" from which to operate. (An elite group of businessmen have put themselves on a "pedestal"; placed themselves above all others; and are conducting business that provides this group with substantial monetary gains; although, what they have given the investor in exchange is a worthless piece of paper.) The investor has, in effect, tossed his money into a black hole (a bottomless pit); dumped money into something which will have no return.

Being fully aware of their self-created position, they are "standing on their toes" (walking on tip-toes) in order to maintain their current wealthy status. They like it where they are and don't want to "fall off."

We see that these Handlers are on the "inside" of this great circular counter and are therefore, protected from any wrongdoing in the transactions that are taking place. They, themselves, will not suffer any losses. These Handlers belong to the "inner circle" of a group of "great" (or wealthy) people.

We also find that I am looking for a swinging gate that would allow these Handlers to navigate "in and out"; push the gate (a device by which to control admission) in either direction to gain entrance, or to exit.

I find no swinging gate; no door; only an opening. This tells us that these people do not have the need to go "in and out." These people are already with the "in" group and have no desire to go "out." They belong to a select group, and feel well "protected" (being on the inside of the circular counter).

If there had been a gate or door that was partially open, then it would indicate that this elite group had been careless by leaving themselves open. But there was no such obstacle to prevent entry; just an opening through which anyone could enter.

The key word here is "careless."

The dream shows us that they were not careless in a true sense, but actually so *over confident*, they didn't even *bother* to put in a gate. Therefore, they have no "controlled admission" anymore.

This means someone from the "outside" can penetrate (get inside) this group and find out what they are doing; can correct this fraud being carried out on the American public. Prosecution of this elite group will be difficult, but not impossible.

In the Stock Market crash of 1929, people had been "buying on a margin" which allowed them to put down only a small percentage of actual money, while the brokerage firm "carried" the rest. This allowed the buyer/customer to purchase a lot of stock for which he never actually paid. The brokerage firm was allowing him to stretch his dollars as far as possible.

Never expecting the market to fail, many buyer/customer's over extended their abilities to pay on demand, and when the market collapsed, they lost everything.

Many committed suicide.

Currently, people can still "buy on a margin," although the laws are more stringent now, in the hopes of preventing another such catastrophe. However, the dream tells us that we do have some problems; the problem being quite different this time.

Last time, it was due to people not putting enough cash down at the time of purchase. This time, even though the monetary safety factor has been increased, it will have nothing to do with what happens next.

When the stocks begin to naturally fall (fail), it will be discovered that MANY of the stocks thought to have value DO NOT EXIST.

There is no symbolism in this interruption!

These stocks have been carefully manipulated to LOOK real, when in fact, there's nothing there.

The buyer/customer's money will have simply vanished into a black hole.

This warning about the "creative" financial maneuvers of the financially elite within our nation is to open our eyes to a manipulative system that has existed for quite some time.

We, the people, can correct this.

My unseen friends want us to think even deeper in terms of the word "stock." They want us to relate it to the American public's belief systems; virtually *anything* that we put "stock" into. That is, anything that we *believe* in; that we have been *told*; that we base our reality on because of what we have been told.

In summation, much of what we "buy" has no truth in it.

And, strangely enough, our own government has the same problem. Much of what it takes "stock" in (holds as true) has been elaborately detailed for them also. They are being manipulated by very powerful persons within our own country, as well as those of foreign soil, who desire control; an *extremely* elite group.

Venturing further into the dream, we are being shown the *old* building as an indication that what is taking place is not new; neither the idea of stocks, nor the type of transactions.

The ornateness of the room tells us that the designers and architects (the creators of this room and its functions) have gone to "elaborate detail" for the comfort and pleasure of the customer (investor). These elaborate details are "to put us at ease."

Why the creators of this room (or these endeavors) have gone to "elaborate detail" to "put us at ease," is disquieting. They want something from us, and they are getting it; according to my unseen friends.

What are they getting from us?

Our hard-earned dollars, for one; but also, a well-trained following of humanity that will do their bidding; whatever that bidding may be.

I don't know how we got ourselves into this mess.

Where did we lose our independence and when?

Did we, the people do this all by ourselves or was it our leaders?

Or, were we possibly manipulated for the purpose of a controlled outcome?

Did you know that in 1908 "Teddy" Roosevelt had the "In God We Trust" removed from our gold coins?

The following year it was put back... but why did he do it in the first place?

If we truly are "one nation under God," as our Pledge of Allegiance indicates, why are we tempting fate?

Why would we boldly remove reference to the trust we have placed in a Supreme Being whose protection we have so heavily relied on?

Is it recorded anywhere that we, the people had a say in this matter of removal?

I stated in the beginning of this book that I would not include references to biblical passages unless they occurred in some extraordinary manner.

This one did.

Shortly after my dream trip to view the buying and selling of stock, I was presented with a passage that began, "Throw away your money!" It is from Ezekiel and happened in the following manner.

For many years now, it had become a comfortable habit for me to keep my Bible on my desk where I wrote most frequently. This being the case, it was not unusual to find this Book of Books open at any one given time. I may well have used it and simply did not close it when through.

On several occasions, within the period of three or four days, I noticed the Bible open as I walked past the room where it lay. Backing up, I would venture to the desk and habitually close it.

I have no idea why.

Having done this repeatedly, I began to realize that I had not used the book; therefore, there was no reason for it to be continuously open.

This particular Bible was exclusively mine; no one else in the house used it.

Now, the next time this happened, it occurred to me that I may have failed to observe something important and this time, took careful note of the opened pages, marking the page numbers on a pad of paper.

This action took place three (3) different times and it was always the same two pages. It was obvious that a specific message was being delivered within the depths of these two pages in front of me.

I read what I was directed to read from my Oxford Annotated Bible, but chose more modern terminology from the Living Bible for recording the warnings in my notebook. Again, the Force is unhappy with us.

Throw away your money! Toss it out like worthless rubbish, for it will have no value in that day of wrath. It will neither satisfy nor feed you, for your love of money is the reason for your sin.

Prepare chains for my people, for the land is full of bloody crimes. Jerusalem is filled with violence, so I will enslave her people. I will crush your pride by bringing to Jerusalem the worst of the nations to occupy your homes, break down you fortifications you are so proud of, and

defile your Temple. For the time has come for the cutting off of Israel. You will sue for peace, but you won't get it. Calamity upon calamity will befall you; woe upon woe, disaster upon disaster! You will long for a prophet to guide you, but the priests and elders and the kings and princes will stand helpless, weeping in despair. The people will tremble with fear, for I will do to them the evil they have done, and give them all their just deserts. They shall learn that I am the Lord. (Ezekiel 7:19 & 23-27)

I believe we can get a pretty clear picture of what the Force is trying to say. It does not intend for us to literally throw away our money like worthless rubbish. The point here is that it will do us no good come those final hours. So, if we have a great love for money and the things money can buy *over and above* all else, we need to re-think our priorities.

Indeed, the land *is* full of bloody crimes and the city *is* full of violence, a story told daily by many of our local, national and international newspapers. Due to our bloody nature, our Creator intends to bring the worst of the nations to take possession of our homes. This does not necessarily mean that an entire army will march in and take over our homes, but it *could* happen. It can be as simple as inhumanitarian acts of terrorism.

We must not underestimate the meaning here!

We are warned that we will be stripped of our dignity, of our pride, of our power. We have already been previously told that we are puffed up with pride, that we are boastful, that we are braggarts.

It is apparent that we think pretty highly of ourselves, and He intends to reprimand us harshly if we do not change. Again, we are reminded that we have an attitude problem.

Our places of worship are to be violated, to be defiled.

We will make petitions for peace, but we will not get it.

Disaster upon disaster will befall us, and we will seek assistance from religious figures, our President and Congress, anyone who will listen; but, they will have no answers; they will be frightened, too.

When some of us were little children, we were taught what was called the Golden Rule, "Do unto others as you would have them do unto you," but not many of us practice that rule today.

Now our Creator says that He will treat us with by the same treatment we have bestowed on others. He will deliver measure for measure. Each action and decision will be weighed, and what we give out, we will receive in return.

He has repeatedly told us that we still have to opportunity to change the ruler by which we are to be measured, but not much.

When darkness comes, it will come swiftly.

Chapter 18

NOW IS THE TIME TO PRAY

The year had already been quite good to me and continued to look extremely promising. It was late summer, 1987.

I had remarried in the Spring and could not help but wonder what new adventures were in store for me because of this special partner who understood not only the new Heaven and Earth of which I have spoken, but readily accepted the existence of Beings, other than human, that visited this Earth as well.

I was finally at peace with myself and life in general. I loved my new home on the prairie where fox, coyote, antelope and rabbit made brief appearances.

Our ivory colored, brick house was solidly perched on a moderate hill where panoramic views of distant mountains could be readily seen from anywhere within the yard or through selected windows from within the house.

One of my favorite rooms in this ranch-style house was the Sun Room, which was given to me for sewing projects and writing. It was a simple room with one small window and a wall of sliding, glass doors which led out to a narrow, concrete walkway near my vegetable garden.

The sliding glass door afforded me with not only a view of my garden, but a spectacular vista of mountain peaks, sloping hillsides, and a beautiful, stately pine tree that resided more towards the front of the house than the side.

There was a wide, carpeted area in front of my desk that separated my writing arena from the brick wall on the opposing side of the room. The indoor/outdoor carpeting provided ample tidiness for the main portion of the house caressing dirty shoes and sandy feet as they ventured in from the sandbox, yard and various garden areas.

I placed no pictures, or ornamental objects on that brick wall to provide a more simplified atmosphere in which to write; mountains and trees were all I needed for decoration. This unheated Sun Room was my refuge; a place to escape; even if only for a little while.

It was on one of those days of retreat, that found me sitting in the Sun Room at an angle behind my desk, admiring the majestic mountains in the distance. I was aware of my comfortable surroundings which included a typewriter, my sewing machine, cabinets filled with miscellaneous treasures, and an untidy arrangement of books.

As the sun streamed through the sliding glass door to bathe me in a blanket of warmth, I turned my face more upward to include the stately pine tree that was positioned in the right-hand corner of my vision. I closed my eyes briefly and began to sense the presence of my unseen friends.

I was told to look at the brick wall in front of me, and in doing so, opened my eyes to a blank wall that soon changed dramatically. As the scene was being staged for me, for the first time ever (in the case of visions), I lost all sensation of being in that room, or at the desk. I was visually transported just outside this room to my vegetable garden where I patiently stood facing west; towards the mountains. I was already in the vision:

VISION... **It is broad daylight. My eyes are lifted skyward to the Heavens filled with fleecy white clouds against a dull blue sky. I feel dizzy as I watch the clouds whiz by from left to right, but know that the clouds themselves do not cause this.**

Sadly, I realize that my beautiful Earth is listing; rolling over on her side like a distressed ship in a mighty sea. My Ship in the Sky, my planet, is dealing with her problems the only way she knows how; adjustments are necessary.

I know her concerns are not for her visitors, neither human or animal, for they never die; they merely shed their outer garments and travel elsewhere with no need for the baggage of a body.

Earth is uncomfortable, and without permission from her visitors, simply rolls over in her bed of endless blue and settles into a more comfortable position.

All things were restored and I was once again seated behind my desk. I had just witnessed the Earth settling into a new position as she encircles our great sun.

Just before I saw the clouds whiz by, I sensed a brief halting in her body, as though she was holding her breath; she stopped rotating. Then, she careened a bit, rolled over, settled into her new position and began breathing and rotating once more.

Sensing her new position, I would say the Earth relocated by a minimum of twelve to fifteen degrees.

Since the clouds were rushing by from left to right, and I was facing approximately west, it means the Earth was rolling in a more southerly direction as seen from my perspective; my perspective being Littleton, Colorado in northern Douglas County.

Clouds rushed by, rather than stars, which is additional information indicating that the action will occur during the daylight hours in America. On the other side of the world, of course, our fellow Earthlings will be in the dark.

Was this what the Beloved disciple, John, made reference to in the Christian's Book of Revelation when he spoke of stars falling from the sky; after which there was a new Heaven and a new Earth?

Only time can provide us with that answer.

When the time comes that our lovely Earth rolls over the winds generated by this disruption will blow at incredible rates, well above hurricane force. I am told these winds will be greater than any recorded tornado; more in the neighborhood of 400 miles per hour.

In the meantime, winds of incredible proportions will take place all over the globe as we experience less than subtle changes in Earth's new magnetic fields. These have already begun.

After the new tilt occurs, when we look up into the night skies, the stars and planets that we have become so accustomed to observing will no longer be there to guide us. We will have to search wholeheartedly for star clusters that produce familiarity in order to gain a better perspective as to our position within our own solar system. North, south, east and west will not be the same. Watching the sun rise from our newly rotated position will be a shock for all of us, but we must quickly learn to adjust.

It will be at least a couple of years before we can count on replenishing our food supplies with a good growing season; the seasons now being considerably different in all locales. Climate adjustment will be dictated by new wind patterns, Earth's new tilt toward the sun, new water configurations and significant land and soil modifications.

It will take the large water masses multiple years to settle down making boat and ship travel impossible. Crossing the mighty Mississippi River will be unthinkable for years; perhaps, as many as five to ten, due to its treacherous waters and massive increase in width. This river will develop into an enormous inland sea, severing the eastern portion of America from the west.

For us, the Atlantic and Pacific oceans, of course, will not be navigable for an even longer period of time. This my unseen friends have made very clear. The newly modified oceans and seas will have much to contend with from the severe volcanic activity within these watery basins causing great turbulence. The enormous winds will not allow for calmness, either.

As to air travel... something new will be used. Our conventional aircraft will be useless. I hesitate to say this, but... the craft I was shown was elongated; completely unlike anything we currently use; more hot dog or cigar shaped, but shorter. This craft used a fuel foreign to anything we presently use either commercially or privately in our planes today.

I believe it was hydrogen; a water-based fuel.

Not long after this vision, my oldest daughter, now called Bobbi; my husband, Greg and I were working out by our barn. It was late in the afternoon and we were aware that a cold front was scheduled to move in, so each one of us anxiously worked to complete our allotted chores before the weather changed.

Bobbi was rummaging through dusty cardboard boxes and plastic trash bags looking for children's clothing. A family "in need" was expected to arrive later in the day to pick them up. Greg was making major repairs to the barn door, and I was pruning the lilac hedge.

I was getting tired, and in a less than gentle manner put the misshapen pruning shears down on one of the railroad ties bordering the hedge. I took off both garden gloves and lightly tossed them onto the open tailgate of our truck.

Taking the path towards the barn where Greg and Bobbi were still working, I felt a cool breeze as it crept around my sandal-covered feet and moved on to parts unknown.

"I think that cold front's moving in," I casually mentioned as I walked up to Greg, "I can feel the coolness already."

"How much longer before you get the barn door fixed?" I inquired nonchalantly.

"Not much longer," came the reply.

The breeze increased in intensity and the playful whirlwinds around my dusty feet suggested that heavy sweaters might soon replace our flimsy summer attire. Not uncommon in Colorado.

"I really don't feel like working anymore," I said suddenly recognizing my total weariness, "I'm gonna put my gloves and tools away."

I stepped away from the barn and noticed that the smell on the wind forewarned of a strong northern breeze. This was evidenced by the "perfumed" stockyard odor which always accompanies breezes from the north; not that they have ever been particularly offensive; but a smell we rarely detect being so far away.

I looked north by northwest towards the front range of the mountains and gasped, "Oh, my God!"

"Mom! What's wrong?" Bobbi called as she hurried to my side. Greg was right behind her.

"Look at that!" I exclaimed staring wide-eyed and pointing with an accusing finger.

A wall of dust and debris several hundred meters in height was rolling down the valley that lay between the front range to the west and the high, sculptured plains to the immediate east. This wet-sand colored mass rolled over and over on itself like a tidal wave that never hit its targeted shore line, but raged on to consume its unsuspecting prey.

"Oh, my God, Mom! Where are my kids?" Bobbi questioned with obvious concern.

"They're all inside," I announced with confidence.

"Let's get everything inside quickly before it hits," Greg demanded more than suggested.

I had no problem in scurrying about to complete the specific tasks as I desperately wanted to spend more time in observation of this powerful display by Dame Nature. I wanted to feel her force from a spectator's seat of safety within the confines of the barn.

My mind was racing to recall something that seemed familiar as we secured all areas... I had seen this before!

Where had I seen this before?

The impish breezes turned into a full scale wind that had little regard for anything in its path. All manner of light-weight objects came sailing by as this rude wind bore them skyward. The air grew cooler and cooler reaching a capacity that could be considered downright cold within a matter of minutes.

It hit from the north with full impact as I stood protected on the south by the barn.

I watched in sheer fascination as our enormous, one-ton truck shuddered when it was struck broadside by blasts of dirt-filled air. The sound was like sleet, striking not only the truck, but the barn, fence, trees, house, and everything within reach.

The wooden barn gave a slight moan as she took her hit in stride.

The lawn chairs we had left around the pool were tossed off their feet and rocketed to new positions, while the trees bowed greatly at the request of these unforgiving forces.

The cold front had definitely moved in!

I relay the above story as a foundation upon which to tell you of a similar event. It concerns another dream of warning that the above storm brought back to memory.

DREAM... **I am awakening from what appears to have been an unconscious state and sense that all is not well. My mind seems to be analyzing the body, going over every part. It concludes that all is well; yet, I have no desire to open my eyes at this point. I choose to listen first, in hopes of gaining a better perspective as to what has taken place.**

As I listen acutely, I cough and become aware that my chest... no my lungs... are not comfortable.

I cough, again.

Breathing is difficult.

I recognize the smell of what I am breathing from working with my dad in building houses... it is dried concrete, but mixed with dust!

The deathly silence that greets my listening ears makes me even more uncomfortable. I hear something large fall disturbing the dust and dirt around me, causing me to cough again.

I have not moved *one bit*. With great caution I slowly open my eyes, and with the realization that I am not in any immediate danger, assess my surroundings. I very slowly rotate my head to get a better idea of what I should do next.

Something tickles my face, and I slowly raise my hand to brush it away only to find that I am absolutely filthy; covered in fine dust particles.

Reassuring myself that I can move without pain and complication, I begin to literally crawl on my hands and knees through rubble, heading toward a place where I believe a door used to be; not that a door serves any useful purpose at this time.

I find I am in the remains of a basement whose upper structure no longer exists.

Still somewhat dazed, I reassess my surroundings and sense these surroundings are the remains of a garden apartment or condominium complex. Timber is strewn around at random. Fortunately, nothing seems to have struck me.

I feel the need to get out and look for someone. At this point in time I do not know who. I am concentrating on careful maneuvers to get me out of this mess caused by some terrible disaster.

I emerge unscathed, stand up and gaze about in confusion and utter disbelief as I slowly and unthinkingly brush the dirt and dust from my clothes.

Looking about, I scarcely recognize the landscape!

It looks like a tornado has been at work, but as I am thinking this I know that it was *not* a tornado.

I am too shocked to think.

Huge, broken pieces of concrete and twisted steel are everywhere!

I find myself stepping over all manner of items, including people and animals.

Can't think!

Must think... am heading towards... Winni!

I am looking for my youngest daughter, Winni, and her two boys.

The place is Arizona!

I get the impression it is Phoenix.

There are very few people, very few; only a minuscule amount. Those who have managed to reach the streets are stumbling through the wreckage like zombies. Of those wandering around, few seem to be in command of their faculties.

The eerie silence of this disaster is frightening.

Not a single whole tree has been left standing. All have been uprooted or snapped in half. Even large hedges have been severed.

Automobiles lie in heaps among the wrecked homes, apartments and broken trees.

Gasoline is pouring out over the streets.

The smell of gas... propane and natural gas... hurts my head.

My nostrils burn.

As I approach the apartment complex where Winni is living, I see a familiar face and inquire as to where I might find her. The man points and indicates that she and the boys are all right.

Upon finding them, they are just fine as the young man had indicated.

Their garden apartment was three quarters underground which provided them with much safety. Their apartment complex was not built as high as the one I was in and therefore, did not suffer the dire consequences of buffeting winds. It is obvious that the Great Wind went right over them and deposited very little debris on the patio and left their sliding glass door intact.

The public park that faces her patio is barely recognizable. The huge chain link fences are scarcely visible, being covered with all manner of things which had been blown up against them. Some fences have been torn down by the sheer weight of the debris. Only stumps of trees remain.

I am still bewildered.

Winni says, "I'm all right, Mother. The boys are just fine. Go tell the people, Mother. Go tell the people."

As I face the park and listen to Winni's words repeat themselves over and over in my mind, someone directs me to walk outside towards the park. I know it is my dream companion. He directs my attention to the right where I hear a distant roar. There I see a HUGE wall of dust and debris moving towards us at an *indescribable speed*.

I know that this is what caused the destruction before.

I know this is the wind that will circle the globe many more times before it quiets down.

I fear it is too late to tell the people; I have waited too long.

I begin to cry.

The roar becomes deafening, the speed overwhelming and the intimidating height of the wall of wind and debris makes me feel faint.

I am absolutely devastated by the scene, and can no longer stand to watch.

My dream companion was standing on the patio with me and when I became too sad to watch anymore, he removed me from the scene.

It was in this dream that I first saw that huge wind-wall of dust and debris, just like I witnessed in my own backyard. It is very frightening to see in "real life" a miniature replica of what you have already seen in a frightening dream.

The dry winds in the dream are more powerful than a hurricane. These winds are the result of the winds getting all mixed up and colliding one with the other as they search for new directions in which to flow when the Earth rolls over on her side. It is clearly to be understood that Phoenix, Arizona will not be alone in the attack of such ferocious winds.

The entire world will be affected.

There is no question in my mind just how much this unseen Force loves us. It is constantly bombarding us with information on what IS taking place, what MIGHT take place, and what WILL take place. All of these messages are designed to alert the children of this planet that their time is running out.

Am I worried that perhaps, many of these predicted events will never come about?

No.

Am I worried about looking foolish if the events do not occur?

No. I am not like Jonah.

I am presenting these messages, just as I was instructed, "whether they hear or refuse to hear"; that is my mission.

Recently another message arrived which was rather odd and left me confused for awhile.

I was extremely tired that morning as I attempted to awaken, and after brief consideration, made a decision to go back to sleep and acknowledge the day later.

As I slipped back to a world of silence, my dream teachers began urging me to do... something.

DREAM... **I am in a rather typical classroom where I am the only student. I am not seated. Whatever I am supposed to do seems to require a standing position.**

My unseen companions, who usually accompany me in my dreams and visions, are scurrying about and have manifested enough for me to physically see them for the first time. I am somewhat surprised at what I see although it does not particularly bother me. Normally, they remain out of sight and simply assist The Advocate in setting the stage for whatever I am to see or do.

There are so many of them present! I have never, ever witnessed, or sensed so many around me before! They seem to be disturbed; not an aspect of their nature I am accustomed to sensing.

I don't understand the cause for their excitement!

It's as though they were not prepared for me to be in that classroom; as though The Advocate brought me there before they were ready. But, this does not bother me either.

I am the student; they, the teachers.

They will "teach" when ready.

The classroom atmosphere having settled down, the Beings are now trying to communicate/convey something to me.

I don't understand.

They are urging me to accomplish... something.

Finally, one of them gives me a fairly large board, perhaps sixteen or eighteen inches high and thirty-six to forty inches long, about three quarters of an inch thick and painted white.

I am also given something equivalent to a black felt-tip marker and asked to write.

Stepping back, the Beings patiently wait for me to write.

Through telepathic communication, I have the impression that only three words are to be written and begin to make my first mark.

With the first stroke of the "pen" (/) I realize I will not have enough room to complete the statement I have been instructed to write.

I am confused.

No advice is given.

I contemplate for some length of time how I might erase; no, "correct" the error as there is no such thing as an eraser where I am.

I am thinking about reconstructing the letters of the first word, which is "NOW," but realize that my slant cannot be used for the second stroke of the "N" nor the third stroke, either.

As I was thinking in the dream about what I should do next to correct the error, something awakened me and I lost my trend of thought.

It was my husband.

He was sorry to have disturbed me, but needed further information before he could continue working on his current project.

The matter was discussed, and within forty-five minutes or so, I was drifting off to sleep again.

The sign board reappeared.

DREAM (continued)... **How could I have been thinking there were only three words to record?**

I realize now, that the message is to read: "Now is the time to pray."

I remember!

Telepathically, I had been given the whole message; however, the language in which I chose to write contained only "necessary" words.

I had confused myself with this written language by the single stroke of my pen.

I was asking my companions how to correct this mistake; I needed some answers.

The message was repeated; and I was further told this message was to be written down; a sign was to be made; an advertisement, so to speak.

This sign was to be for all mankind. It was to be presented to man so he would *know* what he was supposed to do.

Much later in the day, my husband's parents came to the house, bringing over some freshly cooked rhubarb. I thanked my mother-in-law, Berniece for her goodies and for the prayers I knew she had been offering on her son's behalf.

I had pleaded with Greg's mom earlier, for additional prayers for Greg's peace of mind, my sanity, and some worthwhile business dealings to put our income on an upward swing.

Mom had been spending a lot of time in extra prayers and was glad to hear that things were beginning to improve.

I told her about the sign I was directed to make while I was in a dream state, but did not relate the confusion I encountered when trying to record the words.

195

As I completed my story about "**Now is the time to pray**," she held out her hands and extended her arms, inviting her husband, Greg, and me to participate in a communal prayer.

We all chuckled a bit, but did nothing.

How sad!

Were we actually embarrassed to participate in common prayer?

Did we not know what to say?

Is this how the rest of mankind will greet the words on my sign?

After dinner that night, I went outside to pull weeds. Greg was working on new fencing around the chicken yard that housed our feathered friends. These repairs were being done in response to an announcement I had recently made concerning an unusual dinner that would be taking place the following evening.

The main course was scheduled to have the word "chicken" in it, *all eighteen of them*; but, my husband's wisdom prevailed and the chickens got a stay of execution. Greg said we would work something out so the chickens could not venture into the backyard again.

Only the day before I had wandered into my backyard with a pleasant attitude which deteriorated rapidly when I discovered that our family fowl had trespassed beyond their allotted play-yard and stomped, munched, pulled and bedded down in my prized flower beds.

They were lucky to still be alive!

The evening wind began to blow cold and I added the warmth of flannel to my summer wardrobe in order to continue the chore of removing unwanted weeds.

Later, I helped Greg with new fencing and then retreated to the comforts of a warm bath. The water relaxed my body and mind to a point of drifting away.

I don't know where I was headed in my dream world, but I was back in a flash.

Now, I knew why I had been having difficulty in writing the message my companions had given me.

Now, I knew why I had been confused.

Somehow, either because of my companions' language or because of some distant past language I once knew, I was trying to record in "marks"; a written language which used an entirely different format for writing than my current A-Z alphabet.

In addition, this written language did not record unnecessary words such as "that," "they," "we," "to," "you," "an," "and," "is," "the," etc. These "little" words were/are merely inserted at the time of "reading"; never written down; and because of that, the only words I originally felt I needed to inscribe on that board were **Now, Time, Pray**... only three words.

How fascinating!

I additionally wondered, if when I became confused over the mark I had made and did not know how to correct my error, did my Dream Companions use Greg to interrupt my sleep state; giving my mind a chance to re-group?

I'll never know. But, after that brief interruption from dreamland, when I went back into the dream world, I was not longer confused and was able to record the message without delay.

Some may ask, "Who gave you this awareness?"

I would have to reply, it was my dream companions hard at work, once again. It was they, the workers, who were my "teacher's aide" that day. It was they who presented the original dream. It was they, who would also have to provide the required information to eliminate my questions.

What is, or what was, this language that briefly entered my thought patterns and how long ago did it exist, or is it current?

I have no idea.

Shortly after these events took place, The Advocate stated the following:

But know ye all men that God does not warn lightly nor does He joke. Take heed when He speaks and prepare yourselves.

- The Advocate

A little prayerful conversation with one greater than ourselves is desperately needed at this time. Some feel awkward about the whole idea of prayer and have no idea what to say. Others believe some fancy protocol must be followed or the prayer will not be heard, but I find no such evidence that ornate protocol is required for addressing our Creator.

Prayer can simply be looked at as a respectful communication between one greater than us and ourselves. We just need to start talking.

We have been warned many times that the Creator wants to hear some praises from the people of this land. He would like us to "phone" home; let Him know how we are doing, and thank Him for all his past and present help.

Saying a little "thank you" for the future wouldn't hurt, either.

It would be nice to "phone home" and speak to Him while He is still willing to listen.

When you start phoning home, you may think He is on vacation, has His answering machine on, and isn't returning calls... but He is always listening. He is just waiting for the right moment in which to speak to each one of us individually. Maybe He has already phoned us, and it is *we* who did not answer.

I keep saying time is short and I'm sure I am thought of as a doomsday messenger, but I do not wish to see the predicted, dramatic Earth changes occur. Therefore, I will continually appeal to this nation to act swiftly and change what we have been told to change!

So,

NOW is the TIME to PRAY.

Chapter 19

TAKING A STAND

I have had occasion to meet some most remarkable individuals while on my new walk in life with Greg. Many of these people are far more advanced spiritually than I; but, I hope some day to attain their level.

One such woman, of international fame, spoke to a small group of us and explained many aspects of life to which we were relative newcomers. Her communication abilities to access planes beyond our present existence on Earth, are quite remarkable.

She told a group of us that while in a car one day, traveling with a friend, the Christ spoke to her and directed her to "Tell them that I love them." This directive was heard by the friend also.

Now this petite lady spends her life traveling from continent to continent informing man that he is well loved by a power greater than himself.

This delightful daughter of the Most High also told us about visiting some friends in Sedona one evening, and while seated on their porch, looked skyward. As she looked, there were several flickering red and green lights which she recognized as our friends from worlds beyond.

She posed a question to the Beings, and in true innocence telepathically inquired: "Do you know God?"

A thundering reply came back, "We KNOW God. You TALK about God."

The "you," of course, was all inclusive. It referenced the human species.

These Beings seem to know us better then we know ourselves. We are told that we don't know the Creator at all. We just *talk* about Him. We have no personal attachment to our Maker whatsoever.

Jointly believing in a Force greater than ourselves, Greg and I have tried to stay committed to Its service and perform those functions for which we believe we were born.

It has not always been easy.

Firmly adhering to the belief that the more one learns from this Great Force the less that individual is allowed to behave in an unrestricted manner, has caused enormous amounts of frustration at times. We have personally found that the Force will not tolerate waverings from those of Its human team who are fully aware of what they must accomplish.

There are no punishments handed out, but "good things" will no longer fall in their laps like ripe apples from a tree.

Greg knows that his function on Earth is to bring people together; that is, he is to introduce people one to another for the mutual benefit of the introduced individuals.

He performs his job well, never hesitating to pick up the phone and call anywhere in the world if he feels certain individuals would benefit from working together and sharing similar enterprises for materialistic or spiritual gain.

When Greg and I were married he asked me where I would like to ultimately retire, knowing full well that my mind and body required a peaceful abode in which to write? He, of course, would still play the role of "mutual benefactor" to people all over the world, but wondered where the two of us might ultimately conduct our missions together.

At first, I thought the question a little odd since neither one of us was even *close* to retirement age; but, realizing that his question was quite serious, and owing to the fact that I was not crazy about going to Sedona, Arizona (which was his first choice) I replied seriously.

"I have to have trees... trees are my friends."

"Some water... running water."

"Some hills... if I don't have mountains."

"Have to have some game... deer, rabbits.

"Birds... song birds."

"More moisture than Colorado, that's for sure!"

After a long pause I reiterated, "Trees and water! I think they are the most important for my mental state. And, the ability to plant and raise crops; good growing seasons."

"Why do you ask?"

"Well, I thought we might do a little planning, just get some idea of places we might like to go," Greg responded.

Time passed and not much more was said about this discussion related to a place to retire. I had actually forgotten all about it.

Then one night Greg announced that he had found the general location of our future home.

"Where?" I excitedly questioned.

"Nebraska," came the confident reply.

"**NEBRASKA!**" I repeated in utter disbelief.

Nebraska was certainly not a state *I* had in mind!

After he calmed me down, he told me that he had already contacted a real estate agent and had some pictures to show me. I looked at them and was not the least bit impressed.

Nonetheless, plans were made to look at the area... it was the least I could do after all his trouble.

A day was set, and the long drive began. I enjoyed the fact that we were just getting away from the house and realized how seldom we were alone.

Miles before we reached our destination, I began to feel guilty about all the trouble that I had caused this man when he had announced the state of his choice. It was certainly not a state I had *ever* considered as a potential future home having been raised in the East among lots of trees; but, as I watched the surrounding landscape develop into gently rolling hills; saw the rivers, streams and multiple lakes; caught glimpses of the wildlife... my discomfort faded.

Reaching the heavily pined woodlands near our selected town, I knew this would be our home of the future.

We rented a house along the river and drove up to this home-away-from-home as often as we could in pursuit of a homestead we could ultimately call our own.

After two years of steady searching, a small ranch was selected with plenty of trees for me, a spring-fed stream, acres and acres of pasture land, deer, rabbit, pheasant, turkey, hawks and more song birds than I could ever count.

We held a family meeting, where I reiterated the upcoming Earth changes, and Greg and I informed everyone that the land we were about to purchase was for all immediate family members; if they wanted to come. Each one of the children would be allowed to select a homesite. The only request we made was that homes be selectively spaced so that no one person would be looking at another's home; privacy was important.

Returning to Denver after the land contract was signed, Greg and I made a decision to sell our Denver home immediately and consolidate our belongings. Monies would be needed for great quantities of food, warm clothing, adequate housing and to finish paying off the land.

Greg also felt it was imperative for me to get my books out to the people and therefore, told me to leave my government position, knowing that this is what I wanted to do anyway. Whether the house was sold or not, Greg told me to give my employer a date of departure, take what I needed, and head for the ranch immediately.

We both had great concerns that time was of the essence and I needed to complete my work as directed by my unseen companions.

That night as I stood by our bedroom window gazing at the twinkling stars, and vaguely thinking about the contract we had just signed, I realized I was becoming more attuned to the mournful song of the coyotes than my beautiful stars or the recently signed contract.

My ears were acutely listening to the songs of these wild canines, which seemed ever so mournful. Tonight's tones did not carry the usual joyful greetings of fellow pack members mingled with the normal wails as they launched their heads to embrace the dark sky. It caused my own heart to cry with them as I looked to the north and watched the encroachment of civilization as house upon house marched relentlessly across the fields, engulfing the once open range that had been home to the coyote, prairie dog, rabbit, red-tailed fox, antelope, elk, meadowlark and others for more years than man can count.

At one time, in the not too distant past, these creatures shared their platters of grain with man's cattle, and did not mind. There was plenty for all and there was no need to worry about their home life.

Today, it is not the same.

Today, bulldozers bury the dens of these ancient carnivores and force them to seek other pasture lands. The elk, who were originally driven from the prairies to the mountains due to the encroachment of man, are now being forced back to the prairies in search of some solitude and better feeding grounds.

On our subdivision grounds, we have watched for the past two years as herds of antelope wander through the fields between our houses, jumping over fences and meandering short distances over asphalt roads with expectations of new feeding territories.

These gentle pronghorn appearances have always been welcome and met with a certain amount of awe; but, the splendid creatures have paid a heavy price for their attempts to share with man and his domestic animals.

Many are now dead; sacrificed in the name of civilization.

For several days in a row, during a recent summer, scores were killed as they attempted to cross the highway seeking fresher feed plots. I will be glad when we finally move to the ranch where all the creatures are free, and I do not have to witness the demise of such beautiful creations.

Greg and I do not plan to hunt.

The original idea to provide each one of the children with their own space on the ranch changed dramatically when our two daughters considered the purchase of a small farm right next to ours.

We were delighted.

Both girls were divorced with two children of their own, and looking to create better living environments for their offspring. Since they have never had child support from their ex-husbands, a business they could operate from their homes was paramount. This was accomplished.

The land was purchased, and the girls moved immediately to their site. The grandchildren began their education here in a tiny prairie schoolhouse whose total student count was ten; that included Kindergarten through Eighth grades. Four of those students belonged to my daughters.

What an experience for all!

My oldest son recently bought land which adjoins us on the south increasing our expectation of establishing a small community in which we can barter among ourselves and our neighbors; enhancing the special talents of the many rather than the few.

Our ranch is open to a limited number of immediate family, as stated before. Those who are of "like mind" and are earnestly preparing for these imminent changes are welcome to settle nearby.

A contract was finally signed to confirm the sale of our Denver home in mid-December; twelve days before I was to end my government service. We closed in mid-January where the temperature at our new homestead was reported to be a chilly, fifty-one degrees below zero.

All our books on survival materials, food storage, alternative energy, dome homes, etc., were packed in special boxes to be kept close at hand for further research.

All my boxes of reference material and the endless drafts of my books also had specially marked boxes. These were to be among the first items to arrive at our remodeled farm house.

At the time we made a decision to sell our Denver home, we were fully aware of the tremendous task in front of us to consolidate all our possessions from a 4000 square foot home into a 1200 square foot, 1909 remodeled farm house. We knew there would be some difficulties encountered if we tried to stuff furniture, workbenches and shop tools, treasures from the two-car garage, and years of collectibles stashed in the barn into this tiny house and its surrounding "out" buildings. *Much* needed to be sold.

A major garage sale was planned and well executed.

When spring arrived at the ranch, we began planting fruit trees almost immediately and introduced gooseberries, strawberries and high bush cranberries to our newly constructed orchard. We interplanted some asparagus among Mother Nature's wild raspberries, plums, chokecherries and grapes with additional plots of asparagus staked out closer to the house.

Having had vegetable gardens for a number of years, this was a prime consideration when we charted space allocations for areas of special interest. Growing our own food was important to us in whatever form it took. These allotted plots were not necessarily singled out in some square marked off specifically as "the summer vegetable garden." We enjoyed planting lettuce, some herbs, and cherry tomatoes and eggplant among the rash of multicolored flowers that entertained us along the white picket fence. This left far more space in the "big" vegetable garden for veggies that required lots of room to roam.

We experimented with various weed control techniques, none of which included pesticides; some with greater success than others.

As the season marched on, we concluded we had done well in marking out our garden plots. They were well prepared and provided a bumper crop of delectable edibles.

The root cellar was cleaned, painted and new shelves were built to hold tight our treasures of canned and fresh foods.

And yes, we saved our grain.

Seeds had been purchased, used, cleaned, dried and saved for future needs. All hybrids were excluded from our storehouse of seeds as they would not produce with consistency year after year.

Canning utensils and a pressure cooker now line the pantry wall waiting for the next season when they are called into use.

Food dehydrators stand in readiness.

The kerosene lanterns are stacked neatly on the shelves along with the many boxes of candles for emergency light.

Essential tools have been purchased at a variety of stores, through mail order houses, and by means of auctions. A team of plow horses was purchased by my daughter, Bobbi, so that we can learn to plow in preparation for the time when fuel for tractors and trucks will be non-existent.

A milk cow grazes the pasture along with goats, sheep and chickens. Bobbi makes butter, cheeses and even her own soap. She has learned to spin yarn from the hair of the Angora goats, which she has dyed into gorgeous, brilliant colors. From these she has made mittens, socks, sweaters and blankets; and is hoping this spring, to include bison fibers from a neighboring farm in some of her newly designed crafts.

Herbal remedies for healing are her real specialty.

We, Greg and I, have made our start; we have acted on behalf of the warnings from my unseen companions, and committed ourselves to do our best to survive and to assist other human beings. We are dramatically changing our attitude about many things and doing our utmost to remember to say "Thank You" more often to a Force greater than ourselves.

We want to be a part of the new world.

There is still much my husband and I have to do, and while doing them, will keep both friends and family informed of every new dream, vision and message.

And My Creation shall vomit forth its venom and man shall flee in terror as My wrath shall be made known.

~ THE FATHER ~

THE FATHER again speaks of His anger. Very specifically He is talking about the volcanos He created, and the havoc that they will bring down upon mankind. Man will indeed flee in terror. But there will be few places to go. Preparations to flee should have been made long ago.

When the volcanos erupt they will affect people all over the world. The major effect will not be the lava and explosions themselves, but the heating up of the atmosphere which will cause deluges of rain.

Remember the rains that were forecast when we were told to "**save your cereal.**"

I tell you this, people of America: Mt. Rainier is scheduled to blow her top around the turn of the century, and along the California/Nevada border is a caldera of immense proportions growing rapidly. This great, smoldering entity will erupt very soon.

The entire world will have unprecedented food shortages due to the dramatic weather changes. As hot ashes are hurled into the air, and the Earth and sky heat up, the winds will be altered. The ashes will cause a temporary blockage of the sun's light. Massive quantities of rain will be everywhere.

Crops will not grow.

People and animals will have difficulty breathing. Hordes of insects will descend on the land, torturing both the lovely Earth and its inhabitants.

These are the times we have been told to prepare for.

We have been warned!

Whitley Strieber in his book, COMMUNION stated that he did not actually believe the world would end, but could easily be convinced that our biosphere would soon change dramatically, resulting in an enormous loss of human life.

For ease in understanding the term "biosphere," I turned to The WORLD BOOK Encyclopedia which explains the term as follows: "All the Earth's animals and plants live on the Earth's surface or close to the surface -- underground, underwater or in the atmosphere. The region where life is found is called the Earth's biosphere.

It has been a long time since The Advocate first gave me the command to "**write**" and "**record**." He has been my constant companion and loyal friend all these years. He is still here, my mission is not yet complete, but I have now been given permission to close the pages on this, the first book I have been called to write.

The once innocent child has grown up a lot!

She has been educated well.

In her wildest dreams she could never have foreseen the magnificent adventures that would be hers to experience, nor could she have known the companionship that would develop between herself and a Presence beyond this world; a Presence that many may say, doesn't exist at all.

But I, personally, know this Presence; I know It exists.

It is with me everyday.

In honor of Its loving kindness, and as designated "watchman" for this America, I will continue to "**write**" and "**record**" whenever "they" speak.

I will not ask "why?"

I will simply obey.

Selected Bibliography

Gailey, Phil "Officers Agree With Calley Verdict" *The Atlanta Constitution* newspaper, March 31, 1971.

Gailey, Phil "Didn't Kill Wantonly...Calley" *The Atlanta Constitution* newspaper, March 31, 1971.

_____ *The Atlanta Constitution* newspaper, September 13,1970.

Nebraska Rural Electric Association *Rural Electric Nebraskan* magazine, Lincoln:

Steinhart, Lawrence M. *Edgar Cayce's Secrets of Beauty Through Health*, New York: Berkley Medallion, November, 1976.

Stern, Jess *Edgar Cayce - The Sleeping Prophet*, New York: Bantam Books, Inc., January, 1968.

Strieber, Whitley *Communion*, New York: Avon Books, February, 1988.

CONTACTING THE AUTHOR

The author may be contacted through
Coleman Creek Publishing at the following address:

COLEMAN CREEK PUBLISHING
575 N. Main Street
Valentine, NE 69201

To order additional copies of **TO WHOM IT MAY CONCERN: BOOK I, Many Are Called,** complete the information below.

Ship to: (please print)
Name _____
Address _____
City, State, Zip _____
Day phone _____

____ copies of **Many Are Called** @ $14.95 each $ _____
Postage and handling @ $2.95 per book $ _____
NE residents add 4½% tax $ _____

Make Checks Payable to ***Coleman Creek Publishing***

Send to: Coleman Creek Publishing
575 N. Main Street ❈ Valentine, NE 69201

To order additional copies of **TO WHOM IT MAY CONCERN: BOOK I, Many Are Called,** complete the information below.

Ship to: (please print)
Name _____
Address _____
City, State, Zip _____
Day phone _____

____ copies of **Many Are Called** @ $14.95 each $ _____
Postage and handling @ $2.95 per book $ _____
NE residents add 4½% tax $ _____

Make Checks Payable to ***Coleman Creek Publishing***

Send to: Coleman Creek Publishing
575 N. Main Street ❈ Valentine, NE 69201